D1566390

COURTS OF TERROR

Courts of Terror

SOVIET CRIMINAL JUSTICE
AND JEWISH EMIGRATION

by Telford Taylor

with Alan Dershowitz, George Fletcher,
Leon Lipson, and Melvin Stein

ALFRED A. KNOPF · NEW YORK
1976

DS
135
R92
T4

Five counsels who handled arguments against indicted German officials in Nuremberg, 1946. Left to right: Auguste Champetier de Ribes, France; Thomas J. Dodd, U.S.A.; Sir David Maxwell-Fyfe, Great Britain; Roman Rudenko, U.S.S.R.; Telford Taylor, U.S.A.

Some of the American attorneys who have been working to help Soviet Jewish prisoners. Left to right: Eugene Gold, Melvin Stein, George Fletcher, Telford Taylor, Alan Dershowitz, Leon Lipson, Nicholas Scoppetta. (Wagner International Photos)

Contents

APPENDIXES

viii   Contents

Preface

This book is not a study of a general subject, but the story of
a project. The purpose of the project was to obtain relief for
a number of Jewish (and two gentile) citizens of the Soviet
Union who had fallen afoul of Soviet criminal law, and
been convicted and imprisoned, in the course of their efforts
to emigrate to Israel. The means used by the group of American lawyers engaged in the project comprised a presentation
to the Soviet authorities of violations of Soviet law committed by law-enforcement officials during the trials and in the
prisons, in the hope that such a showing would induce those
in higher authority to reconsider the sentences and alleviate
the conditions of confinement.

Thus, although the book involves both Soviet criminal
justice and Jewish emigration from the Soviet Union, it does
not deal with either as a general subject. We consider here
only a handful of the hundreds of thousands of criminal
trials held annually in the Soviet Union. The victims of the
abuses perpetrated in these particular proceedings number
less than a hundred—a wholly insignificant figure even in
terms of today's diminished stream of Jewish emigration.

Nevertheless, in both of these dimensions the significance
of the trials far transcends the numbers directly involved. In
any country espousing the rule of law, the true quality of a

judicial system is best measured by its resistance to stress, whether caused by community, racial or other prejudice, or by the pressure of State political policies and interests. In these cases the Soviet State had a strong interest in condemnation and punishment, and it applied pressures which badly fractured the rules for the conduct of trials and the confinement of prisoners. The consequence inverted the old saw; bad law made hard cases—indeed, scandalous miscarriages of justice.

The reason why the trials were conducted as they were was exemplary. It was State policy to discourage Jewish emigration without appearing to prohibit it. Loss of jobs, apartments, and other privileges or necessities of Soviet life discouraged some but by no means all would-be emigrants. Use of the criminal law was another and more drastic means to the same end.

Some Jews gave the authorities the opportunity by unlawful attempts at flight, as in the Leningrad case involving the attempted seizure of a small airliner in order to escape to Sweden. In other cases, where there was no such excuse, criminal charges were fabricated. Whatever the basis of the accusations, the State had a governing interest not only to ensure conviction and punishment of the accused, but to warn other potential emigrants that they might meet a like fate.

For this latter purpose, unfair trials were more effective than fair ones. If Soviet Jews came to realize that for them the legally established procedural safeguards were meaningless, and that once charged conviction was a matter of course, the deterrent effect would be that much greater.

Accordingly, this book may be regarded as an account of the prostitution of Soviet justice to serve State ends. Since we hope it will interest lawyers professionally as well as the public generally, we have included generous extracts from the individual petitions and the full text of memoranda on four legal issues which were common to a number of the cases. All these were submitted to and accepted by the Soviet legal authorities.

Many people, some of whom prefer anonymity, joined me in the project, which provides the core of the narrative, and some of these have also contributed to its text. All of us hope that this story is not yet ended, and that its publication may in some way aid or comfort the victims of these abuses, and their friends and relatives who trusted us to do our professional best in their behalf.

—TELFORD TAYLOR

New York, October 1975

COURTS OF TERROR

1

The Trials

In Ryazan, an old Russian town 125 miles south of Moscow, there is a university which has for some years been an educational haven for minority nationalities of the Soviet Union who have difficulty gaining admittance to institutions in the larger cities. The University of Ryazan includes the Institute of Radio Engineering, and during the late 1960s two young Jewish brothers from the Ukraine, Yuri and Valery Vudka, and a slightly older youth from Lithuania, Shimon Grilius, were part of its student body.

Yuri, the elder brother, had an unusually bold and far-ranging mentality. He soon became the leading spirit of a small group, including these three, which initially interested itself primarily in political and economic questions. In time, their activities and interests became increasingly dominated by their Jewish heritage, and they began studying and circulating Hebrew textbooks and encyclopedias, tape recordings of Leon Uris's *Exodus,* Randolph Churchill's *The Six Day War,* and other works of primarily Jewish concern, and essays by Yuri Vudka on various issues of the day, including anti-Semitism in the Soviet Union. In 1969 the Vudkas and Grilius obtained invitations from relatives in Israel, the prerequisite for applying for permission to emigrate.

In August 1969, shortly after these efforts to emigrate had

commenced, all three were arrested, as well as three other members of the group. Their lodgings were searched, and all books and documents with a political or Jewish flavor were seized; from Grilius's apartment in Klaipeda* they took not only Yuri Vudka's memorandum favoring emigration rather than assimilation for Soviet Jews, but also records of Jewish songs, a typewriter, and a painting of a Jew.

The six were charged with violation of Articles 70 and 72 of the Criminal Code of the R.S.F.S.R.,† which proscribe "anti-Soviet agitation and propaganda" and "participation in anti-Soviet organizations." Their trial before the Ryazan District Court was conducted by Judge Matveyev; the heavy atmosphere was lightened by a touch of low comedy when the prosecutor (a man named Dubtsov) introduced a copy of Bertrand Russell's attack on Soviet anti-Semitism, which had been found in the possession of one of the defendants. Ignorant of the illustrious author's identity, Dubtsov misread the name, and vehemently castigated the defendants for their contact with those anti-Soviet scoundrels "Bertrok and Rossel," to the better-informed judge's great embarrassment.

On February 19, 1970, the Ryazan court sentenced Yuri Vudka to seven years' confinement, Grilius and Oleg Frolov (a Russian part-Jew) to five years, and Valery Vudka (at twenty, the youngest of the defendants) to three years. The two other defendants, who "confessed" fully and apparently had caused the arrests by reporting the group's activities to the KGB (Soviet security police) received suspended three-year sentences. On appeal to the Supreme Court of the R.S.F.S.R. these judgments all were affirmed, and the four were assigned to the labor camps for "political" prisoners in the Mordovia region, near the town of Potma.

* Grilius had by this time graduated from Ryazan and returned to Lithuania, where he was employed as a radio engineer in Klaipeda (formerly Memel).

† Russian Soviet Federation of Soviet Republics—the constituent "republic" of the Soviet Union in which Ryazan is located.

While these events were taking place in Ryazan, somewhat comparable proceedings were occurring far away in Bendery, a small city in the Moldavian S.S.R., on the Dniester River some thirty-five miles southeast of Kishinev. Here two Jewish schoolteachers, Josif Meshener and Yakov Suslensky—less philosophical but more inclined to public remonstrance than the Ryazan group—had sent letters to Leonid Brezhnev and the Central Committee of the Communist Party in 1968 criticizing the sending of Soviet troops to Czechoslovakia and protesting Soviet support for Iraq, where Jews were being hanged. They also taped, and played for friends, recordings of "Voice of Israel" and other international broadcasts, and composed but did not send a letter to the United Nations complaining about the difficulty in the Soviet Union of studying the Hebrew language or Jewish faith.

On January 29, 1970, Suslensky's apartment was searched; the tape recordings, the draft of the letter to the United Nations, and his diary were seized, and he was arrested. Two weeks later Meshener was arrested, and both were charged under Article 67 of the Moldavian Criminal Code, the local equivalent of Article 70 of the R.S.F.S.R. Code. They were tried in Kishinev in October 1970, and in his summation the prosecutor requested sentences of three years for Meshener and five for Suslensky. Upon conviction, however, Meshener was sentenced to six and Suslensky to seven years' imprisonment (the statutory maximum), and both were sent to a Mordovia labor camp.

The Ryazan and Bendery-Kishinev trials were the first in recent years known to our group (no doubt there were others) in which the accusation of circulating anti-Soviet propaganda was invoked against Jews for the possession of "Zionist" materials. In both cases, the accused were critical of Soviet policies outside the Jewish sphere, but in neither was there evidence of desire to overthrow the Soviet regime; Meshener, indeed, was a member of the Communist Party.

Neither trial attracted much more than local attention,* but they may be regarded as immediate precursors of the major trials in which Jews seeking to emigrate were convicted of criminal offenses and became, as they are known in Israel, "prisoners of conscience."

The First Leningrad Trial

The story of the Leningrad "hijacking" of June 15, 1970, revolves around two groups of Soviet Jews, one in Leningrad and the other in Riga. Both were Zionist in their outlook, and most of the members in each had made repeated and fruitless applications for permission to emigrate to Israel. The Leningrad group, which had coalesced in 1966, was the larger and better organized; it conducted several *ulpans* (schools) where Jewish history and Hebrew were taught and circulated a substantial quantity of Jewish literature. Most of its members were highly trained scientists, engineers, and physicians in their thirties. The Riga Jews, considerably younger, included students and technicians.

Sometime late in 1969 a leading figure in the Leningrad circle, Hillel Butman, became acquainted with Mark Dymshitz, a former airline pilot working as an engineer in Leningrad. Dymshitz had a passion for flying, and blamed his failure to get employment as a pilot on the fact that he was Jewish. His interest in Jewish culture appears to have been slight, but he wanted to emigrate, and early in 1970 he put to Butman a plan for escaping the country by hijacking a Soviet TU-124 airliner flying the Leningrad–Murmansk route, which Dymshitz would then pilot to Sweden.

Initially attracted to this unpromising venture, Butman interested in it two other Leningrad Jews, Lev and Mikhail

* Neither trial is mentioned in William Korey's *The Soviet Cage* (1973), in which the Leningrad, Riga, and Kishinev trials of 1970–71 are described in detail. Accounts of the Ryazan trial may be found in *Jews in Eastern Europe* vol. IV, no. 7 (Nov. 1971), pp. 205–8, and Schroeter, *The Last Exodus* (1974) pp. 135–39.

Korenblit, and then took Dymshitz to Riga, where they met with Silva Zalmanson, her husband Eduard Kuznetsov, and other members of the Riga Zionist group, a number of whom (including two gentile friends of Kuznetsov) declared themselves willing to participate. An attempt was scheduled for May 1, but before that time Dymshitz took an opportunity to ride in the cockpit of the fifty-passenger TU-124, and decided that it was too large to be flown by a single pilot. Meanwhile, Butman and the Korenblits had had second thoughts, and were urging Dymshitz to give up the plan, which they now saw as illegal, impractical, and dangerous to the Soviet Jewish cause.

But Dymshitz was not to be stopped, and the Riga group—younger, more impulsive, and perhaps more desperate to emigrate—was still ready to follow his lead. Early in June he devised a new plan, involving a smaller airliner, the twelve-passenger AN-2, flying from Leningrad to Priozersk, a small city north of Leningrad and forty miles from the Finnish border. The Riga circle would buy all the seats so that no other passengers would be endangered, and the plan was to subdue but not harm the two-man crew, and leave them on the ground at the Priozersk airport, where four more of their group would be waiting. Dymshitz would then fly the plane with the entire group to Sweden, where they would abandon the plane and ask for asylum.*

As events proved, the Soviet authorities had advance knowledge of the plan in all its details. On June 15, 1970, Dymshitz and his party were arrested at Smolny airport before they reached the plane, and the four waiting at Priozersk were picked up several hours earlier. On the same day, Butman and several other members of the Leningrad group were also arrested, and a number of Jewish homes in Moscow, Riga, and elsewhere were searched and Jewish

---

* The participants thus numbered sixteen in all: Dymshitz, his wife and two young daughters, ten Riga Jews, and the two gentiles. They were too numerous to board the plane at Leningrad, and so were split into two parties as described above.

literature was confiscated. During the next few weeks the arrests and searches spread to Kishinev, Kharkov, and Odessa.

On December 15, 1970, Dymshitz and ten of the Riga participants in this affair were brought to trial before the Leningrad Municipal Court.* There was at that time no Soviet criminal statute specifically applicable to hijacking; the major charges brought against the accused were preparing or attempting to commit treason, and theft of State property on a large scale, as well as anti-Soviet agitation and propaganda. All were found guilty of attempted theft, and all but one (Mendel Bodnia, who cooperated with the prosecution) of attempted treason.

The sentences, announced on December 24, were exceedingly severe. Dymshitz and Kuznetsov, who had already served seven years for "anti-Soviet" activities unrelated to Zionism (Kuznetsov's father was a Russian gentile, and his passport in fact identified him as "Russian" rather than "Jewish"), were condemned to death. Kuznetsov's two gentile friends, Alexei Murzhenko and Yuri Fedorov, had also been previously imprisoned for "anti-Soviet" conduct; they were sentenced to fourteen and fifteen years respectively. Josif Mendelevich, a twenty-three-year-old science student, was also given fifteen years, and the others received terms ranging from thirteen years for Leib Knokh to eight years for Silva Zalmanson's younger brother Israel, and four years for the cooperative Bodnia.

The death sentences caused an international furor, with protests from a wide variety of sources, including the Italian Communist Party. Pressure for commutation was intensified by the Christmas season, and by General Franco's commuta-

---

* Dymshitz's wife and two daughters were not charged, nor was Meri Knokh, the pregnant wife of Leib Knokh. Vulf (brother of Silva) Zalmanson, then serving as a lieutenant in the Red Army, was tried separately by a military court, which sentenced him to ten years' imprisonment.

tion on December 30 of the death sentences imposed on some Basque nationalists whose trial had been violently condemned in the Soviet press. The impact on the Soviet authorities was effective to the extent that the defendants' appeal to the Supreme Court of the R.S.F.S.R. was heard on December 29—only five days after the Leningrad court's judgment—and the Soviet prosecutor himself asked for commutation of the death sentences. On December 31 the Supreme Court affirmed the convictions, but commuted Dymshitz's and Kuznetsov's sentences to fifteen years, and reduced by a few years the sentences of Mendelevich, Knokh, and Altman.

As of this writing, all of the defendants except Silva Zalmanson, who was released for unspecified reasons after serving about half of her ten-year sentence, and Bodnia are still in the labor camps.

The Second Leningrad Trial

Butman, the Korenblit brothers, and six other members or friends of the Leningrad group were put on trial in the "Second Leningrad" case. It was precipitated by the hijacking episode, but only Butman and Mikhail (the younger) Korenblit were charged with criminal culpability in that connection. They and all the others were accused of anti-Soviet agitation and organization; four of them were also charged with complicity in the theft of a government-owned duplicating machine.

Butman and Korenblit had been involved in the first of Dymshitz's plans, but had soon changed their minds and sought to dissuade Dymshitz from further efforts. Butman had gone on vacation away from Leningrad before the final plan was conceived. Nevertheless, both were convicted of attempted treason. All eight were found guilty under the other charges, although the literature which was seized in their homes and relied on as proof of "anti-Soviet" propaganda was plainly Jewish-Zionist rather than revolutionary in character.

On May 20, 1971, the Leningrad court sentenced Butman to ten and Mikhail Korenblit to eight years, and the others to terms of five years or less. All of these were confirmed on appeal by the Supreme Court of the R.S.F.S.R.

The Riga and Kishinev Trials

The Riga and Kishinev trials in May and June 1971 were, essentially, efforts by the Soviet authorities to portray the Leningrad hijacking affair as the product of a far-flung Zionist conspiracy, by associating Jewish groups in those cities with the Leningrad defendants. This was sought to be accomplished largely by newspaper publicity, since judicially the effort failed for lack of evidence, and none of the defendants in either case was charged with culpability in connection with the hijacking. All four defendants in Riga and all but one of the nine in Kishinev were accused of anti-Soviet propaganda and organization. All but one of the Kishinev accused were also charged with complicity in the theft of the same duplicating machine which had figured in the second Leningrad trial and which was alleged to have been stolen from an "institute" in Kishinev where the defendant Rabinovitch was employed. To lend color to the supposed connection with the hijacking, three of the Leningrad Zionist group—David Chernoglaz, Anatoly Goldfeld, and Hillel Shur—were brought to Kishinev for trial with the six local Jews. Shur flatly refused to participate in the proceedings, on the ground that the Moldavian court had no jurisdiction over him.

In both trials, the charges focused principally on the literature and objects found in the defendants' homes. In general, these were the same books and documents that had figured in the Leningrad trials, descriptive of Israel and its history and people, instructive in the Hebrew language and Jewish religion, or analytic of Jewish problems in the Soviet Union.

Except for Chernoglaz and Goldfeld, who received sentences of five and four years respectively, the Kishinev defendants were given terms of two years or (in the case of Rabinovitch, who was charged only for theft of the duplicator) one year. Compared to the Leningrad punishments, the Riga sentences were also light; the heaviest was three years, two others two years, and the fourth one year. At the time this project began, Chernoglaz and Goldfeld were the only defendants from these trials still in confinement, and by the late summer of 1975 all had completed their sentences and been allowed to emigrate.

The Individual Trials

Since the four trials for which, with or without basis, the Leningrad hijacking attempt furnished the primary theme and motivation for the prosecutions, there have been no more group trials. There has, however, been a continuing sequence of individual trials of Jews whose efforts to emigrate, or other activities indicative of devotion to Jewish religion and culture, made them *personae non gratae* to the local authorities. Such trials have occurred in many regional capitals and outlying cities of the Soviet Union, including Sverdlovsk, Vinnitsa, Kiev, Rostov, Derbent, and Kharkov. The amount of information concerning such proceedings available outside the immediate areas varies greatly, and no doubt there have been other comparable trials of which we know nothing.

A number of the Jews involved in these cases might well be described as "activist" or "militant," in the sense that they had repeatedly made themselves obnoxious to the authorities by petitions, letters of protest, demonstrations, and the like. Others appear to have done nothing more than apply for emigration papers, to account for the official hostility to which they were subjected. In all the cases with which our project is concerned, there was either a gross exaggeration of some peccadillo used as the basis for a criminal charge, or the accusation was a complete fabrication.

Favorite tools of the authorities are charges of "malicious hooliganism" and "oral defamation of the Soviet State and social system," under—respectively—Articles 206(ii) and 190–1 of the R.S.F.S.R. Criminal Code, or the equivalent laws of other Soviet republics. Neither charge calls for documentary proof, and both are easy to support by contrived testimony. Thus, in November 1973, Alexander Feldman of Kiev was sentenced to a three-and-a-half-year term for "hooliganism," committed by knocking a cake out of a woman pedestrian's hands and addressing her obscenely. Earlier that same year, Lazar Liubarsky of Rostov was given a four-year term under R.S.F.S.R. Code Articles 190–1 and 75. The latter provision proscribes "divulgence of state secrets," and the accusation was based on an episode five years earlier when Liubarsky, a design engineer, had been reprimanded for showing a confidential sketch of a power station to the chief accountant of the institute where both were employed, in order to support his estimate of the cost. Both Feldman and Liubarsky were inveterate petitioners and protesters.

Perhaps the most repulsive example of this sort of judicial oppression is the case of Isaac Shkolnik, a mechanic (fitter) in an automatic-appliances factory in the Ukrainian city of Vinnitsa. At the time of his arrest in July 1972, it was well known that he and his family were awaiting the necessary *vyzov* from Israel so that he could make application to emigrate.

When arrested, Shkolnik was charged with circulating defamatory statements about the Soviet State, an offense which carried a maximum penalty of three years. Soon it was changed to anti-Soviet agitation and propaganda, punishable by up to seven years. But worse was in store. Shkolnik, though not formally educated, had an active and inquiring mind, and had befriended some English engineers who had been working in Vinnitsa in 1968. English magazines and letters, and a visiting card of one of the engineers, had been seized when his apartment was searched, and after about six months of pretrial confinement Shkolnik was charged with treason by spying for the British government.

When the British authorities categorically denied this, Shkolnik was finally brought to trial on the accusation of spying for Israel. Since there was no shadow of evidence that he had ever met or communicated with any Israeli agent, and there was no documentary evidence whatsoever, the prosecution relied on the preposterous notion that Shkolnik, who had only elementary mechanical training, had been memorizing technical details about the plant where he worked, for the purpose of selling the information to the Israeli authorities if and when he reached that country.

Shkolnik was tried by a military court and sentenced to ten years' imprisonment. On appeal this was reduced to seven years. Apart from the crass fabrication which is manifest from the succession of charges and their egregious implausibility, there were other flagrant violations of legal procedure. Shkolnik is currently confined in a political prisoner labor camp near Perm, in the Urals, where, unless relief is granted, he will remain until April 1980.

2

The American Legal Defense Project

Soviet policy with respect to Jewish emigration has been generally oppressive, but also erratic. One of its features, which I found surprising in relation to the obvious purpose —to discourage emigration by the use of fear—is that the relatives of the Jews convicted in the trials just described have almost uniformly been allowed to go to Israel.* Thus Dymshitz's daughters, the wives of Butman, Mikhail Korenblit, and two other defendants in the second Leningrad trial (Kaminsky and Yagman), and the wives of Chernoglaz and Shkolnik, to mention only some, have all found haven and a new nationality in Israel.

Furthermore, the same is true of the defendants who have completed service of their sentences. Without exception, all of those who have sought to emigrate (and that is very nearly all of them) have been allowed to do so within a few months after their release from confinement. Consequently, by the time this project was inaugurated in the fall of 1973, most of the Kishinev and Riga defendants, and several from the second Leningrad trial, as well as Valery Vudka from the Ryazan trial, had also arrived in Israel.

---

* A possible explanation is that relatives of prisoners and dissidents have often been the source of publicity unfavorable to the Soviet regime, and therefore the authorities are relieved to have them out of the country.

This means that between 1971 and 1973 a considerable number of former prisoners, and relatives of both present and former prisoners, came into Israel. Naturally, there were discussions among them of ways and means to win release or lesser relief for their comrades and relatives still confined in the Potma, Perm, and other camps. Many of the immigrants were well educated, and understood enough of the Soviet legal system to be aware of many respects in which Soviet norms had been violated in the trials. So, too, they were aware of the extent to which the Soviet defense lawyers, for reasons that will presently appear, had been unable or unwilling to press to the full the arguments that might have been made in their behalf.

Early in 1972, Sima Kaminsky (wife of Lassal Kaminsky, sentenced to a term of five years in the second Leningrad trial) and Mindel Veingel (sister-in-law of Chernoglaz) arrived in the United States, seeking aid for the imprisoned Jews. They had no specific plan, but one of the ideas which they put forward was that American lawyers might undertake a professional effort to lay before the highest Soviet legal authorities a showing that these trials had been conducted in flagrant disregard of the Soviet Union's own laws, and seek relief for the prisoners on that basis.

By remarkable coincidence, the same thought had occurred among a small group of lawyers in New York City. The beginning of this group went back to 1967 when, after the Six-Day War, diplomatic relations between Israel and the Soviet Union were severed, and it was widely reported that Soviet Jews were increasingly subjected to harassment of various sorts. Two lawyers—Burton Roberts and Carl Vegari—went to Russia to investigate and report back.

Continuing and increased activity, however, started in 1970, in consequence of the first Leningrad trial death sentences, and the prospect of more trials of Jews in Riga and Kishinev. The nucleus of the group at this time included

Melvin Stein, associate general counsel of the Equitable Life Assurance Society; Allen Schwartz, a New York attorney; and Eugene Gold, the district attorney of Kings County. During the spring of 1971 Gold and Robert Leonard, prosecuting attorney of Flint, Michigan, visited the Soviet Union and had audiences with Soviet officials in Moscow, Leningrad, Kishinev, and Riga. Funds for travel expenses were met by members of two synagogues in New York City. Subsequent trips to Russia, intended to impress on Soviet officials the depth of concern in American legal circles, were made by Nicholas Scoppetta, commissioner of investigations of New York City; David Goldstein, a New York attorney; and others.

Meanwhile, Stein and Schwartz had conceived the idea of a legal challenge by American counsel to the validity of the Soviet criminal proceedings. Stein conveyed the thought to Jerry Goodman, executive director of the National Conference on Soviet Jewry, the organization sponsoring the visit by Sima Kaminsky and Mindel Veingel. Realizing that his guests and the Stein group had independently conceived the same project, Goodman arranged a meeting of Gold, Stein, and Schwartz with himself, Phillip Baum of the American Jewish Congress, and the two women from Israel. Stein has described what followed:

> From the moment we were introduced to the relatives, the meeting was a moving one. Each of the young women greeted us with a friendly handshake and the softly spoken words, "I am Sima Kaminsky (Mindel Veingel), from Leningrad." I think I am being accurate when I recall that this simple identification of name and place had the effect of transporting me, and I am quite sure the others, across distance and time. We were instantly united with our imprisoned brethren more than an ocean away. And we were conscious, too, of a unique historical setting: Through our lives to that point, we had often heard and read of the centuries-old oppression of our coreligionists in the Soviet Union. Now, we were suddenly a part of

it, close to those who had suffered it, and with an opportunity perhaps to do something about it.

As I recall, we sat down to the meal, and were told by Goodman that the women had suggested that lawyers in the United States be enlisted to assist the Jewish and non-Jewish prisoners of conscience whose arrests had been followed by the Leningrad and other trials. Gold, Schwartz, and I presented our own thoughts to the relatives. The idea was that a distinguished legal team would carefully probe the background of the trials and inquire into Soviet law, in order to ascertain the extent to which the trials may have violated the very laws under which they were conducted. To the extent that this inquiry demonstrated serious shortcomings in the trials (and from what we already knew of the trials, we felt that the Soviet authorities had indeed violated their own laws), we would seek to prepare a careful and thoroughly professional legal case. The case would be presented to the Soviet government in quiet and dignified fashion. If that succeeded, all well and good. If not, the results of the inquiry ought to be made public.

The relatives were most desirous of such a project going ahead. They believed that the Soviet government was extremely sensitive to criticism that it did not adhere to its own laws. Gold, Schwartz, and I agreed that we would attempt to put together a team for the legal effort we had discussed. . . .

Not long after, we were informed by authorities on Soviet Jewry matters that quiet diplomatic efforts were being undertaken by the United States government that might accrue to the benefit of the prisoners. It did not seem to be advisable, at that time, for our project to move ahead. Based upon this advice, we held our efforts in abeyance.

In the summer of 1973, more than a year after we had met with the relatives, the hoped-for relief for the prisoners had not materialized. It seemed as if our project should move forward again.

My own first knowledge of the project came in September 1973, from Nicholas Scoppetta, whom at that time I knew as a fellow member of a tennis group at Columbia University's

Baker Field. Subsequently I met with him, Stein, and Gold, and was asked to join them in putting the plan into effect. I was told that Alan Dershowitz, whom I had first known as a student at the Yale Law School and who had since become a professor at the Harvard Law School, would be available as a colleague, and that through him we might also obtain the aid of lawyers versed in Soviet law, of which I was lamentably ignorant.

It soon became clear to me that, for this project, the most important Soviet official was the Procurator General. His functions correspond in some respects to those of the United States Attorney General, though the Soviet official has, at least on paper, somewhat wider powers. Most importantly for our purposes, he has supervisory authority over the work of trial prosecutors and the administration of labor camps and prisons, and can initiate reconsideration of criminal convictions. Since the early 1950s the Soviet Procurator General has been Roman Rudenko, who had served as the Soviet chief prosecutor at the first Nuremberg trial in 1945 and 1946. During that time I was associate counsel on the American prosecution staff, headed by Supreme Court Justice Robert H. Jackson, who had assigned me to act as liaison officer between the American and Soviet staffs—a duty which had involved frequent meetings with General Rudenko. It was agreed that my past acquaintance with Rudenko would at least assist in getting direct access to him to present our case against the trials.

The novelty of the project gave me pause, but on reflection I concluded that the undertaking was well worth exploration. Available literature about the trials raised grave questions concerning their legitimacy under Soviet law, and the humanitarian appeal was strong. Anyone truly interested in his profession is likely to be attracted to situations that raise rare and profound issues and unusual tactical problems. It appeared probable that the undertaking would involve travel to both Israel and the Soviet Union, and contacts with interesting people, whether friendly or hostile to its aims. Furthermore, some of the Soviet lawyers I had met at Nuremberg had been competent and open to arguments of principle and consistency. It was a long shot, but worth trying, so I told Melvin Stein that I would join the group, and pursue their plan at least to a point where its content and promise could be better assessed.

Shortly thereafter, Arkady Voloshin, one of the Kishinev defendants who had served out his two-year term and then been allowed to emigrate to Israel, visited the United States. Stein, Scoppetta, and I met with him, and the interview was exceedingly valuable, not for what we learned about his trial, but for what we found we would need to have and to know in order to conduct meaningful interrogations. For in fact none of us knew enough about Soviet criminal law to ask more than a few pertinent questions, and as to these few, language problems obstructed precision of response.

Plainly, we needed expert legal and linguistic collaboration, and thanks to Alan Dershowitz, it was soon forthcoming. Professor George P. Fletcher of the law school at the University of California at Los Angeles, a specialist in Soviet criminal law and that year a visiting professor at the Harvard Law School, joined the group, and soon he and Dershowitz produced (with the aid of Harvard colleagues) a number of memoranda on Soviet criminal procedure.

At first, enlightenment added to our problems. The idea, so basic to the American system, that the record of a trial and the judgment rendered are public records open to anyone to examine is quite foreign to the Soviet system, wherein these records are closed to public view,* and even the parties may find that access to them is denied. The judgments of the trial and cassational (appellate) tribunals were unavail-

---

* In this respect the Soviet system is not unique. In England the record of a trial cannot be examined without permission of the appellate court empowered to review the judgment. See Taylor, *Crime Reporting and Publicity of Criminal Proceedings,* 66 Col. L. Rev. 34, 50 note 70; Kennedy, *The Trial of Stephen Ward* (1964) pp. 9–10.

able, except for fragments which had been smuggled out of the Soviet Union and which were not only unofficial but bootleg. Soviet press accounts were, of course, officially "inspired." Although under Soviet law the trials were supposed to be "public," in practical effect they had been closed to press, foreigners, and the general public, and conducted before selected audiences. Usually the close relatives of the defendants had been admitted, but in some instances even this basic right had been denied.

There was also the question of our authority to assume the status of counsel in the situation. We knew that some of the prisoners' relatives wished American counsel to act, but their thought had been that we would represent the defendants. That appeared to me to be impossible. It was not merely that we were not members of the Soviet bar. More important, we had no contact or means of communication with the prisoners, all of whom had been represented in their trials and appeals by Soviet lawyers. We could not simply fly into Moscow and declare that we were representing the prisoners, when we had no evidence whatsoever of such authority.

These considerations led inevitably to the conclusion that the first major steps must be taken in Israel. The relatives wished for action, and they were certainly aggrieved and injured by the loss of consort, comfort, and support of their imprisoned parents, husbands, and other kin. In the sense of the American legal concept, they plainly had "standing" to go to court. We could go to Israel and meet with them, and could undertake to represent relatives who wished to give me authority, by power of attorney, to seek relief.

But unless there was a case to be made, in the long run this would have been cruel comfort to prisoners and relatives alike. And by now it had become apparent that the only place where such a determination could be made was, again, Israel. There were to be found the defendants who had served their sentences and been allowed to emigrate, and the relatives who had been allowed to attend the trials and, at long intervals, to visit their kin in the labor camps. Except for the few smuggled fragments of the judgments, these people were the only available source of information on what had happened, from arrest to conviction and in confinement. Obviously, they were interested sources, but there was no other available. And so, by the late fall of 1973, we all had concluded that a trip to Israel was the next and essential step.

3

Gathering the Information

On December 30, 1973, George Fletcher and I arrived in Israel to interview and consult with the relatives and former prisoners. Arrangements for meeting with them were made by the Public Council for Soviet Jewry in Tel Aviv, under the direction of its vice-chairman, Zalman Abramov, and Yoram Dinstein, professor of international law at the University of Tel Aviv. The council also furnished interpreting and stenographic services; the former were more necessary to me than to Fletcher, who had considerable command of both Russian and Hebrew.

We put up at the Plaza Hotel in Tel Aviv, where we were joined a few days later by Alan Dershowitz, and thereafter by Jeanne Baker, a Boston lawyer who had previously been associated with Dershowitz in litigation and had agreed to join our project. We remained in Israel about ten days, and throughout that time we were conducting interviews, dictating notes, and consulting on the significance of what we had learned and what needed to be followed up to round out the picture.

We interviewed, of the relatives, Knokh's wife, Dymshitz's elder daughter, Mendelevich's sisters, and the uncle of the Zalmansons from the first Leningrad trial; the wives of Butman, Kaminsky, Yagman, and Mikhail Korenblit from the second Leningrad trial; the wife of Chernoglaz from the Kishinev trial; the father and the brother of Grilius from the Ryazan trial; and the wives of Markman and Shkolnik. Of the former prisoners, we saw Lev Korenblit, Dreizner, and Boguslavsky from the second Leningrad trial; Shur and Levit from the Kishinev trial; and Valery Vudka from the Ryazan trial.

All these individuals had either been present at their relatives' trial or had themselves been the defendants. They were laymen, but generally they had learned enough about Soviet procedure to describe the trials and call our attention to features in which the defendants' rights had been disregarded. These accounts were numerous enough so that cross-checking and comparison could establish that some of these features had been common to all or most of the trials, and thus an overall pattern soon emerged.

Virtually without exception, the arrests were made coincidentally with a search of the arrestee's home, together with the seizure of all documents or things having any connection with Israel or Judaism, letters from abroad, and instruments of communication, including typewriters. The arrestee was then held incommunicado, usually for the maximum of nine months permitted by Soviet law, before being presented with the formal charges and given access to his dossier. During that time he would be interrogated at great length, as would others thought to be possible witnesses.

The foregoing was generally in accordance with Soviet procedure as prescribed by statute, but what followed was not. Soviet law gives defendants the right to counsel of their own choosing. But when the prisoners' relatives set about finding counsel, they soon discovered that in "political" cases—as these were officially regarded—lawyers would not be allowed to act as defense counsel unless so authorized by a special permit, called a *dopusk*. Consultations between defendants and their counsel were severely restricted in time, closely monitored, and the lawyer was usually not allowed to make written notes about the contents of the dossier.

There were more unpleasant surprises when the cases came up for trial. By statute, Soviet trials are generally open to the public. But the authorities saw to it that, except for the accused's relatives (and in some cases even they were excluded), the audience was "packed" with Communist Party faithfuls invited for the occasion, and others seeking to attend were turned away. Many or most, and sometimes all, of the defendants' requests for witnesses were denied. In the cases where distribution of anti-Soviet literature was charged, the courts presumed the documents relied on by the prosecution to be anti-Soviet in character and would not consider arguments or evidence to the contrary.

These were violations common to a number or all of the trials; there were also those which were unique. For instance, when Mikhail Korenblit, called as a witness in the first Leningrad trial, appeared to be about to say something embarrassing to the prosecution, court officers hustled him from the room, and the defense lawyers were never given an opportunity to question him. The use of the treason statute in the Leningrad trials was a transparent and groundless device to enable the court to impose heavier sentences.

Some of the Soviet defense lawyers represented their clients forcefully, while others advised their clients to plead guilty, and would do little more for them than urge extenuating circumstances. Perhaps the latter were more shrewd than timid, for the boldness of some appears to have availed their clients little, while those who displayed contrition fared better. There were few of the latter, for most of the defendants were conscientiously motivated, and except for the participants in the airplane-hijacking attempt, they believed they had done nothing in violation of Soviet law. No doubt these experiences with Soviet counsel were in part responsible for the relatives' later idea of obtaining American legal assistance.

Nearly all the defendants, after conviction, were sent to the labor camps for "political" prisoners near Potma in Mordovia, or Perm in the Urals. Among the other prisoners there were a few monarchists, Ukrainian and Baltic separatists, and other offbeat dissidents. But the majority were men who had been convicted for collaborating with the Nazis during the Second World War. The Jews, few in number, were easily victimized by these numerous and virulent anti-Semites, some of whom had been in the camps for years, and had become "trusties" of the camp officials. Regulations governing rations, mail, visits, work quotas, and other pains, penalties, and privileges of prison life were constantly applied in a discriminatory way against the Jews, who inevitably fell into disciplinary difficulties and suffered additionally, by long months in solitary confinement, denial of visiting privileges, and in other ways.

Especially unhappy was the plight of the prisoners who had become rigorous in the observance of Jewish religious practice with regard to dress and diet. These included the Vudkas and Grilius, Chernoglaz, and Mendelevich. The Vudkas and Chernoglaz were intransigent to the point that the authorities haled them before local "people's tribunals," who ordered their transfer to the prison in Vladimir, where the regimen was even more rigorous than in the labor camps.

By the time we had been in Israel a week, it appeared clear to me that there was indeed a strong case under Soviet law to be made against the validity of the trials and the conditions of confinement, and that we should endeavor to put our project into execution. Since it was not without international overtones, it seemed to me that the State Department should be informed. Accordingly, on January 3, 1974, I waited on the American ambassador, the late Kenneth Keating, and gave him a full description of the project and its progress up to that time.

The last few days were spent organizing and dictating our notes of the interviews, which we planned to embody in affidavits to be executed by the relatives and former prisoners who had given us relevant information. We also prepared a form for power of attorney, to be signed by the relatives who wished us to represent them. Since it seemed both unwise and inappropriate to appear in the interest of any prisoner without such authority, we had decided to act only in those cases in which an available relative wished to authorize us to do so.

After our return to the United States, the affidavits and powers of attorney were prepared, largely by Jeanne Baker, and sent to Israel for execution. In the upshot, we received powers of attorney from Israel to seek relief for seventeen prisoners—seven from the first and four from the second Leningrad trial, Grilius and Yuri Vudka from the Ryazan and Chernoglaz from the Kishinev trial, and Azernikov, Markman, and Shkolnik. In addition, we were able to establish contact in the Soviet Union with the wives of the two gentile prisoners, Fedorov and Murzhenko, and received powers of attorney from both of them. By the spring of 1974, accordingly, there were nineteen cases in all to be handled.

4

Moscow: April 1974

After the trip to Israel, our group was greatly strengthened by the addition of Professor Leon Lipson of the Yale Law School. Fluent in the Russian language, Lipson is one of the recognized American experts on Soviet law.

Although we now had the information on the basis of which, we believed, strong briefs against the judgments could be written, the crucial question still remained: How could and should it be presented? As foreign lawyers, we had no right to appear in Soviet courts. It seemed most unlikely that any Soviet lawyer would agree to take our briefs and present them as his own, or sponsor them in some other way, and even if such a lawyer could be found, we doubted that such a channel would be at all effective. Furthermore, in all of our cases the judicial process had run its full normal course, and reconsideration would require some extraordinary means.

Soviet law does, however, make provision for postconviction review of criminal cases by a procedure called "judicial supervision." Two of the three highest legal officials of the Soviet Union—the Procurator General and the President of the U.S.S.R. Supreme Court*—are empowered to "protest" a criminal court judgment on various grounds, including

* The third is the Minister of Justice.

substantial violations of criminal procedural law and incorrect applications of substantive criminal law. Such a protest can result in reconsideration of the judgment protested, or even termination of the entire proceeding. Since the Procurator General and President are authorized to act on their own initiative, there appeared to be no reason why we could not seek permission to submit our papers to either or both of them, asking them to exercise their discretion and authority to protest the judgments against our prisoners on the basis of the errors which our papers would demonstrate. Furthermore, the Procurator General is vested with full supervisory powers over all places of confinement, and is made responsible for the observance of all the regulations governing prison conditions and for the elimination of abuses.

We already knew that the Procurator General was Rudenko, with whom I had worked at Nuremberg. I had not previously realized that the President of the U.S.S.R. Supreme Court was Lev Smirnov, who had been a senior member of Rudenko's staff at Nuremberg, where we had not had much professional contact but a pleasant enough nodding acquaintance.

While there was no legal obstacle to either of these officials receiving our papers, they were certainly under no obligation to do so. In fact, I thought it rather unlikely that they would, but there did not appear to be any equally hopeful avenue.

How best to approach them? I was reluctant to write from America, explaining the object of my wish for a meeting, lest I should be told that a visit to the Soviet Union for that purpose would not be welcomed and that no visa would be granted. I was equally unwilling to get an ordinary tourist visa, go to Moscow armed with our briefs, seek audience on a personal basis to renew old acquaintance, and then pull the briefs out of my dispatch case. That would have been undignified on my part, and might justly have appeared to my hosts as an imposition on their hospitality. Furthermore, there was no reason to put our group to the considerable burden of preparing briefs, without some assurance that someone in authority would receive them.

In view of all the circumstances, I concluded that it would be best to endeavor to see Rudenko and Smirnov before preparing the briefs, and obtain their agreement to receive the documents. On March 15, 1974, I wrote to each of them, stating that I hoped to be in Moscow from March 29 to April 6, and asking for a meeting "to renew our acquaintance and discuss questions of mutual interest professionally." The letters were not answered, but George Fletcher and I had no difficulty in obtaining visas for a business trip to Moscow, where we arrived on Friday, March 29, and were given rooms at the Rossia Hotel. Alan Dershowitz and his son Elon, traveling independently, had reached Moscow a day or two earlier.

The day after our arrival I called at the American Embassy to inform them of the purpose of our presence in Moscow (which was already known to them in consequence of my call on Ambassador Keating in Tel Aviv) and ask their assistance in making appointments with Rudenko and Smirnov. Quite properly, the embassy took no position on the merits of our undertaking, which was essentially a private one, but throughout both of our visits to Moscow, Melvyn Levitsky of the embassy staff was most helpful in making appointments for and otherwise assisting us.

No replies from Rudenko or Smirnov were immediately forthcoming, and on Monday, April 1, Fletcher and I went to the Procuracy, situated nearby at Pushkinskaya Ulitsa 15A, to leave a note for Rudenko telling him that we were at the Rossia and would await word from him. On this occasion we were taken to the office of a Procuracy official named Tsibulnik, whom we knew to have received other American visitors in the past, and who appeared to function as a sort of buffer between foreign callers and higher officials of the Procuracy. He told us only that Rudenko was temporarily indisposed and resting in the country, and that he would let us know later whether an appointment could be arranged.

The following day we paid a similar visit to the Supreme Court of the U.S.S.R., and while delivering the letter to the receptionist were told that Smirnov had recently suffered a stroke. (Rudenko later told me that Smirnov was recovering, but we never saw him.)

By Thursday, April 4, there still had been no word from Rudenko. It was an especially tedious wait, because either Fletcher or I had to remain by our hotel telephone in case a call should come. In the evenings we were at liberty, and were able to hear a symphony concert, and attend the Bolshoi Ballet and a performance of Rimsky-Korsakov's *Pskovitianka,* an excellent opera very rarely performed except in Russia. But time was running short, for we were due to leave Moscow on Saturday.

However, the letter to Judge Smirnov paid off, for although he was unable to see us, he was so thoughtful as to ask the secretary general of the Association of Soviet Lawyers, Mr. Galouchko, to call on us at the Rossia. When he arrived late on Thursday afternoon, Fletcher and I explained the purpose of our trip and the subject we wished to discuss with Rudenko.

Galouchko was the soul of courtesy, but it was plain that he was less than delighted by what we told him and regarded the matter as very prickly. He agreed to pass on the information to the Procuracy, but expressed doubt that Rudenko would return to Moscow before our scheduled departure.

Friday, April 5, was to be our last full day in Moscow, and by midafternoon, when no further word had come, Fletcher and I had given up hope and were resigned to going home empty-handed. Fletcher had been eager to spend some time in the bookshops, there seemed no reason for him to hang by the telephone any longer, and around four o'clock he left the hotel.

About an hour later my telephone rang, and my few words of Russian were just sufficient to give me understanding that the caller was the First Deputy Procurator General, M. P. Malyarov. But I was quite unable to converse, and an interpreter called me back a few moments later to tell me that Rudenko was still unwell but Malyarov would receive me at the Procuracy as soon as I could get there. It was suggested that I bring an interpreter.

There was no way to reach Fletcher, so I obtained an interpreter through Intourist (a middle-aged man who spoke excellent English, obviously selected for the occasion instead of one of the pleasant young women who serve as Intourist guides) and went with him in a taxi to the Procuracy.

Malyarov, a square-cut and rather harsh-looking man in late middle age, received me with entire civility but no show of pleasure.* He apologized for Rudenko's inability to see me, and we took up the business in hand with no further preliminaries. He heard me out with only a few interruptions. "So an American lawyer comes to Moscow representing Soviet citizens?" I answered, blandly enough, that I did not represent the prisoners but rather the relatives in Israel. To this there was no verbal reply, but a sardonic smile. "How did you obtain your information about these trials?" I explained that it came from relatives and former prisoners. "What makes you think it is reliable?" I replied that we had cross-checked as carefully as we could, and added that I would welcome an opportunity to examine the trial records, if they could be made available to me. This suggestion was curtly rejected: "You have your way of doing things, and we have ours." I concluded by stressing my desire to proceed in a professional manner and without

* Andrei Sakharov has written a vivid account of his meeting with Malyarov in August 1973. Sakharov, *Sakharov Speaks* (1974) pp. 179–92.

publicity, leaving him to draw his own conclusions about what our course of action might be if he refused to receive our documents.

Malyarov was not disposed to discuss the particulars of the cases. He declared very firmly that the trials had been conducted entirely correctly, and gave me absolutely no encouragement that our suit would meet with any success. He told me that our submission could not be made part of the official record of the proceedings. But in the end he did give me permission to submit petitions in behalf of the prisoners, and agreed to receive and consider them.

This was as much as I had hoped for and more than I had expected. At least our papers would not be "returned to sender," and the work of preparing them would not be wasted. We returned home with a measure of satisfaction that we had at least gained access to the highest levels of the Procuracy, and we were eager to exploit the opportunity thus afforded.

5

Preparing the Defense Case

When Dershowitz, Fletcher, and I returned from Moscow, the law-school semester was drawing to a close. All three of us, as well as Lipson, were heavily occupied with teaching commitments and were unable to start systematic work on our cases until mid-May.

Thanks largely to Alan Dershowitz, we were able to concentrate our activities at the Harvard Law School. On Monday, May 20, our task force gathered, with office space, stenography, and library facilities provided at the school. Dershowitz, Fletcher, Jeanne Baker, and I assumed the main burden of the legal work, with the collaboration of two Russian-trained lawyers (who prefer to remain anonymous), and two young New York attorneys, Joseph Feit and David Shakow. Lipson came from Yale as often as his schedule permitted, to review the results of our work.

We had nineteen cases, and decided at the outset that we would file a separate petition concerning each of the nineteen prisoners. But there were several legal issues, or groups of issues, that were common to all or a number of the cases, and to avoid unnecessary repetition we supported the petitions with four legal memoranda on these matters.*

* These memoranda are reprinted in full in Appendix C, pp. 132–57.

The first dealt generally with the "right to a defense" in Soviet law, with primary emphasis on the consistent denial to these prisoners of the right to counsel of their own choosing. The second was focused on the cases involving the charge of anti-Soviet propaganda (R.S.F.S.R. Article 70), and violations of Soviet procedural law in adjudicating the anti-Soviet character of literature seized from the accused. The third was concerned with conditions of confinement in the labor camps and Vladimir prison. The fourth was devoted to the charges of complicity in treason and the large-scale theft of State property, of which the defendants in the first Leningrad trial, and Butman and Mikhail Korenblit in the second, were convicted.

This last issue was the key to the heavy sentences received by Butman, Korenblit, and the first-Leningrad-trial defendants. Dershowitz undertook to supervise the preparation of Legal Memorandum IV and the main body of the petitions in the Dymshitz and other first-Leningrad-trial cases. Fletcher functioned similarly on the other three legal memoranda. I took the Butman case, used it as the vehicle to develop the organization and format for all the individual petitions, and thereafter prepared the petitions in the second Leningrad, Kishinev, and Ryazan trials.

The petitions all asked the Procurator General to do three things, and after the opening formal recitals and factual statements, the body of each petition was divided into three parts, corresponding to the three prayers for relief. The first, invariably much the longest of the three, comprised the arguments in support of the prayer that the Procurator General protest the judgment, on the grounds that it was (as specified in Article 342 of the R.S.F.S.R. Code of Criminal Procedure) "one-sided and incomplete," or in "substantial violation of the criminal procedures law," or based on an "incorrect application of the criminal law." The second was addressed to the Procurator General's responsibility, under Article 32 of the Statute on the Procuracy, for "observance of the rules established by law for the keeping of confined persons," and requested correction of abuses set forth in this portion of the petition. The third was a prayer for executive clemency. This power was constitutionally lodged in the Presidium of the Supreme Soviet of the particular Soviet republic in which the trial had been held, but recommendations or prayers for executive clemency could validly originate either privately or from a government agency, and in effect our request was that the Procurator General recommend clemency to the Presidium of the R.S.F.S.R. or other appropriate Soviet republic.

Treason and Theft of State Property

In the protest part of the petitions, there were two vital points that applied to the majority of our prisoners. The first, relevant to Butman and Korenblit in the second and all the accused in the first Leningrad trial, was that the charges based on offenses carrying capital penalties—treason (Article 64) and theft of State property on an especially large scale (Article 93-1)—were not rightfully applicable to the defendants' conduct. No doubt what the participants in the hijacking project had done was criminal. They had certainly endeavored to leave the Soviet Union "without . . . permission of the proper authorities," an offense punishable under Article 83. They were perhaps guilty of failure to report intended crime (Article 88-1), or of an offense involving misuse of State property (Articles 93 and 212-1). But none of these crimes carried more than a three-year sentence.

Treason under Article 64 requires "an act intentionally committed . . . to the detriment of the State independence, the territorial inviolability or the military might of the U.S.S.R." Plainly, an intent to go to Israel did not meet this requirement, nor did a purpose to seek asylum in Sweden as a step to that end.

The Soviet prosecutors were, of course, aware of this flaw in their case, and argued that the necessary intent was shown by the character of the literature circulated within the Zionist groups. But of course this literature was in no way threatening to the "independence" or "territorial inviolability" or "military might" of the Soviet Union. Furthermore, neither the gentiles, Fedorov and Murzhenko,* nor Dymshitz, more interested in aviation than in Judaism, had had anything to do with such literature.

The convictions based on Article 93-1 were equally ill-founded. As shown in Legal Memorandum IV, "stealing" or "theft" in Soviet law means more than using another's property without permission; it means taking the property with intent to keep it and treat it as one's own. The hijacking project involved no such purpose. The intent was to use the airplane to fly to Sweden, after which it would be abandoned and certainly be repossessed by the Soviet government. As stated above, the project was a criminal one, but not under Article 93-1.

It seems clear, accordingly, that Articles 64 and 93-1 were invoked by the Soviet authorities, despite their manifest inapplicability, in order to subject the defendants to the jeopardy of capital sentences. The spuriousness of these charges is underlined by the fact that Bodnia, who co-operated with the prosecution, was convicted only under Article 83, although he was fully involved in the hijacking project.

Anti-Soviet Agitation and Organization

The second major legal issue concerned the charges under Articles 70 and 72, which were largely based on Zionist and

---

* In Murzhenko's case, the trial court's effort to find treasonous intent went so far as to rely on its own characterization of Murzhenko as not being a "100 percent Soviet man."

other Jewish literature seized from the defendants' homes. These charges were the core of the second Leningrad, Riga, Kishinev, and Ryazan trials, and were also relied upon by the prosecution to show treasonous intent in the first Leningrad trial and the cases of Butman and Mikhail Korenblit.

In a prosecution under Article 70 based on the possession or circulation of literature, it is essential that the prosecution establish that the material is of such a nature as to "defame the Soviet State and social system." Furthermore, the literature must be circulated or possessed "for the purpose of weakening the Soviet regime" or of "committing . . . especially dangerous crimes against the State."

But, as Legal Memorandum II shows, these crucial issues were simply not adjudicated. The reason is obvious: the Zionist literature was *not* of the subversive character stipulated in Article 70, and there was no evidence of the subversive purpose it requires. Instead of proof in court, the authorities inserted in the accused's dossiers an official analysis of the literature, variously described as a *Glavlit* or an *Oblit,** embodying a finding that some or all of the material taken from the defendants was of the character described in Article 70. Thereafter, the issue was regarded as settled; the trial courts would not consider contrary opinion. *There was no trial of the crucial issue.* This handling violated a number of the provisions of the Code of Criminal Procedure, which requires that all evidence relied on by the tribunal be read in open court (Code of Criminal Procedure Article 240) and that the tribunal rely only on such open evidence (Article 301), and which gives the accused the right to challenge expert testimony and call experts of his own choosing (Article 185).

Additionally, the requirement of subversive intent was ignored by the courts in all these cases. It was plain enough that the accused were not seeking to weaken the Soviet re-

---

* An *Oblit* would come from the *Oblast* (regional) authorities in charge of censorship; a *Glavlit,* from the central State authorities.

gime, but rather to practice their religion, to deepen their knowledge of Jewish culture, and to join their fellow Jews in what they regarded as their homeland.

Violations of the Right to Counsel

The other violations of Soviet law and practice were not as standardized as those just discussed, but some of them were almost as pervasive and just as serious. Probably the most important departure from prescribed practice was in connection with the selection of defense counsel. Soviet law explicitly guarantees defendants the right to counsel of their own choosing (R.S.F.S.R. Code of Criminal Procedure, Article 48), but in virtually all of our cases this basic right was flagrantly violated by the requirement that only counsel with the *dopusk* (i.e., permit or clearance) could be retained, and in other ways as well. Butman, for example, though an engineer by profession, was also a graduate of the Leningrad Law Institute. He informed the authorities that he wished to act as his own counsel, a right explicitly guaranteed by Article 50 of the R.S.F.S.R. Code of Criminal Procedure. Nevertheless, a lawyer was designated by the Leningrad Collegium to defend Butman, who was told that he had no right to refuse his services.

Perhaps the most shocking abuse of the right to counsel took place in Shkolnik's case. When his wife initially sought counsel, she was informed that only one lawyer in Vinnitsa, Makarenko, had the necessary *dopusk* authorizing him to handle such cases. She was dissatisfied with his handling of the case, but made no effort to replace him during the trial, and after his conviction she asked Makarenko to take an appeal. When he refused, she obtained the services of a lawyer named Sarri,* recommended to her by the Moscow Collegium. But the prison authorities would not allow

* Sarri had represented Knokh in the first Leningrad trial.

Sarri to see Shkolnik, and Makarenko reappeared and insisted on handling the appeal (which was unsuccessful) even though Mrs. Shkolnik refused to retain him. Subsequent protests by Sarri and Mrs. Shkolnik were ignored by the authorities.

Abuses in Conditions of Confinement

Soviet law with respect to penal sanctions contains many provisions which, most penologists would agree, are admirable. As set forth in a standard work—*Basic Principles of Legislation Pertaining to Correctional Labor in the USSR and the Union Republics*—they stress the corrective purpose of confinement, and repudiate the infliction of physical suffering and the degradation of human dignity. Official regulations are particularly concerned with the health and well-being of the inmates. To ensure observance of these principles and practices, and prevent abuses of all sorts, the Procurator General is given full investigative and corrective authority over labor-camp and prison administrations.

It is, of course, virtually impossible to get a disinterested account of conditions in the Soviet camps and prisons. Furthermore, not all are alike; some are better than others, or, as the less charitably inclined would say, some are worse than others. Our sources were primarily the former prisoners now in Israel and, secondarily, the relatives, most of them our clients, who had visited the camps. They were sufficiently numerous to give us a reasonable basis for confirmation by cross-checking, and the results of our inquiries are set forth in Legal Memorandum III and the affidavits attached to it and to the petitions.

The results speak for themselves, and there is no need to duplicate here what can be read in the affidavits reproduced in the appendixes. Two general features of the treatment accorded the Jewish prisoners, however, warrant emphasis.

The first concerns the difficulties and harassments confronting the prisoners who endeavored to continue in confinement their observance of Jewish religious practice, especially the dietary laws and the wearing of beards and yarmulkas. This, to be sure, is an area in which the record of prison administrations in other countries is by no means impeccable. However, in the Soviet Union the Criminal Code (R.S.F.S.R. Article 143) makes it an offense punishable "by correctional tasks for a term not exceeding six months or by social censure" for any person to obstruct "the performance of religious rites, insofar as they do not violate public order and are not accompanied by infringement of the rights of citizens." Furthermore, the Soviet Union, as a member of UNESCO, voted in 1957 in favor of the Standard Minimum Rules for the Treatment of Prisoners, of which Rules 41 and 42 reflect a policy favoring opportunity for prisoner religious observances, as long as such observances entail no interference with prison discipline. Under these circumstances, it would appear that the labor-camp officials, who forbade the efforts of Mendelevich, Grilius, and the Vudkas to continue Jewish religious practices, and punished them, were acting unlawfully, and that the Procurator General was legally responsible for correction of the situation.

The other feature is the vicious consequence, as described in the affidavits of Shimon Levit and Valery Vudka and confirmed by other camp inmates, of confining the Jewish prisoners in camps where the greater part of the prison population was composed of former Nazi collaborators. According to Valery Vudka, these included former members of the Vlasov forces, composed of Russian soldiers taken prisoner by the Germans and then formed into an army commanded by General Vlasov, which joined with the Germans against the Soviet forces: "Among them was Staplinski, who had been an officer in the Vlasov forces" and

"Another former Nazi collaborator was Balashov." Levit writes in greater detail:

> In Camp No. 3 there were about 450 prisoners. These included eight Jews, and small groups of "Nationalists" (a group which included the Jews, Ukrainians, Lithuanians, etc.), so-called "democratic" dissenters, so-called "Russian Nationalists" (which included monarchists), and a religious group which included Baptists and Jehovah's Witnesses. All these groups together made up about a quarter of the entire group of prisoners.
>
> The other persons, comprising about three-quarters of the total, had all been convicted of crimes committed as collaborators when the German Nazi forces invaded the Soviet Union during World War II. Between that war and my time in Camp No. 3, there had been two amnesties pursuant to which many former Nazi collaborators were released. Those who were still in jail while I was in the camp were serving long sentences imposed because their crimes had included one or more murders.
>
> The Nazi collaborators were given for their work the easier and better jobs, in which the fulfillment of the work quotas was possible. The Jewish prisoners were given the hardest and most unpleasant work, for which the quotas were fixed at an impossibly high level. For example, the Jewish prisoner Vulf Zalmanson, who was an engineer, was at first given technical work in the automobile wheel factory in which most of the prisoners worked. But a few weeks after his arrival, when the camp authorities learned that he was a Jew convicted at the so-called "Leningrad Hijacking" trial, they gave him hard and disagreeable physical labor, with the other Jews. Meanwhile, the Nazi collaborators were given jobs as clerks, security guards, etc., and some of them were referred to as "Brigadiers." The result of these conditions was that the Jews were constantly in difficulty for not fulfilling the work quotas, and lost their privileges in connection with food parcels, visits, etc., while the Nazi collaborators got favored treatment.

Of all the matters I learned while preparing these cases, none surprised me more than or shocked me as deeply as this situation. Furthermore, no other feature of the cases gave me as much reason to hope that Rudenko, given the background of his Nuremberg experience, would be moved to take corrective action. As the remainder of this account will disclose, however, that hope has remained unfulfilled.

6

Moscow: June 1974

In addition to his major contribution to the content of the petitions and memoranda, Alan Dershowitz, with the aid of Jeanne Baker, Feit, and Shakow, took the burden of seeing to the typing, translating, and assembling of what became a virtual mountain of legal material. We had decided to submit everything to the Procuracy in both English and Russian, so that forty-six separate documents* were involved. Russian typewriters and sufficiently skilled translators were in short supply, and at times it appeared that we would fail to meet our deadline of June 9, when Leon Lipson and I were scheduled to leave for Moscow. But by dint of persistence and much night work, everything of importance was finished in time, so Lipson and I were able to leave with a complete portfolio. We arrived in Moscow on Monday, June 10, and were given rooms at the Ukrainia Hotel.

On this occasion there was no difficulty in obtaining an appointment with Rudenko, who sent word through Levitsky at the embassy that he would receive us at two o'clock in the afternoon on Wednesday, June 12. We were shown into the Procurator General's conference room by the chief

* English and Russian versions of nineteen petitions and four legal memoranda.

of his chancery, Vladimir G. Rogovin, where we were joined a few moments later by Rudenko and an interpreter. Rogovin remained in the room during the meeting but did not speak.

I had not seen Rudenko since 1946. He was not greatly changed in appearance or manner, and was wearing an ordinary business suit and a single medal which proclaimed him a Hero of Socialist Labor. He had held his position for over twenty years, and must have handled himself very shrewdly to have survived the political vicissitudes of those many years, including the fall of his fellow Ukrainian and friend, Nikita Khrushchev, whose grave in the Novo-Devichi Cemetery I had seen in March.

Rudenko received me with a cordiality and even warmth which seemed to me entirely genuine. For over a quarter of an hour we discussed Nuremberg and a number of its participants, a subject which turned a bit melancholy because so many of them had meanwhile died. He made no move to end the reminiscing, and it was I who had to turn the conversation to the business at hand.

Since Rudenko had been informed of my previous talk with Malyarov, there was no need for me to retell my whole story. He at once confirmed his deputy's agreement to receive our petitions, but coupled this with a categorical denial that there were any defects in the decisions, and reiterated this several times despite my request that he suspend judgment until he had read our documents. I was finally constrained to remark that there were occasions in the past when I had been quite certain of an opinion but had been persuaded to change it by fresh information. He acknowledged that such might be so in general, but without any sign of open-mindedness on the immediate subject.

At some point Rudenko asked about the source of our information concerning the trials, and when I referred to the affidavits executed in Israel, his manner, for the first and only time, was slightly hostile. Later he lectured me at length on the seriousness of the crime of hijacking, to which I replied, as soon as I could get in a word, that I hardly needed this instruction, especially since it was usually American and never Soviet aircraft that were thus victimized—a reply that produced a guffaw from Rogovin but not from Rudenko. Furthermore, I observed, the first Leningrad defendants had not been convicted of hijacking but of treason, which was a quite different crime. His unguarded answer was that at the time of the Leningrad episode there was no Soviet law explicitly punishing hijacking.* This, of course, was tantamount to an admission that the treason statute had been invoked because a properly applicable statute was lacking.

Throughout the talk, Rudenko spoke as if the participants in the hijacking project were the only prisoners involved, and was either unable or unwilling to speak of the other cases. As with Malyarov in April, I could not engage him in any close discussion of the legal points. Feeling that we were getting nowhere, I turned to the clemency prayers. Rudenko quite properly observed that this authority was reposed in the *praesidia,* but added that the Procuracy would not "play postman" by forwarding our requests. This was wide of the mark, for we were asking him to consider the petitions and make recommendations to the *praesidia.*

Lipson then emphasized that we were not attacking Soviet administration in general, and were seeking to work within their system by calling attention to violation of their own norms. Rudenko brought the business part of the meeting to an end by saying that he would pass the petitions to Malyarov for review, and then give us an answer, and asking us to submit the documents to Rogovin. He then took us into his private office for a few more minutes for social chat, after which we handed Rogovin our forty-six documents.

* Such a law was promulgated in January 1973, with a penalty of five to fifteen years' imprisonment, with death sentence in cases where the crime caused "the death of people or . . . grave bodily injuries."

Before departing, Lipson asked Rogovin how soon we might expect a response, but got no meaningful reply. We told Rogovin that we would remain in Moscow for a week, so as to be available in case our materials required further explanation, and he suggested that we telephone Malyarov the following Monday.

Since there was no need to sit by the telephone, the waiting period was much more tolerable than it had been in April. The weather was generally fine, and we strolled in the Gorki park and visited the home-museums of Tolstoi, Chekhov, and Scriabin. On Sunday we took a tourist bus trip to the old churches and monasteries in nearby Souzdal and in Vladimir, where Yuri Vudka and Chernoglaz were then imprisoned.*

In the afternoon of Tuesday, June 18, we reached Malyarov by telephone. Lipson talked with him and interpreted for my benefit. The gist of Malyarov's statement was that the Procurator General had already told us that there was no error in the judgments, and he, as deputy, had no authority to come to any different conclusion. This, of course, made a mockery of the whole proceeding, and was directly contrary to Rudenko's assurance that Malyarov would review the petitions, and that we would then receive a response based on that review. Answering a question, Malyarov also indicated that there would be no written reply.

Lipson then inquired whether there would be any action on our prayer for rectification of the conditions in the labor camps. Malyarov replied that no special consideration could be given to Jews. The answer clearly showed that either he had not read the petitions or had chosen to ignore their contents, for of course we had not asked any special favors for the Jewish prisoners, but rather that Soviet laws be observed and the discriminatory punishments and harassments to which they were being subjected be stopped.

---

* Since then, Chernoglaz has finished his term and he is now in Israel. Butman, Meshener, and Suslensky have been transferred to Vladimir.

At the end of the conversation Malyarov took pains to emphasize that if we wished any relief for the prisoners, the proper procedure would be for them to file petitions for clemency with the R.S.F.S.R. or other appropriate presidium. When Lipson pointed out that the prisoners were not our clients, Malyarov replied that we should tell the relatives who had retained us to pass that information to the prisoners.

There was nothing more to be accomplished in Moscow, so we informed Levitsky at the embassy of the course events had taken, made our travel arrangements, and departed the following day.

7

Soviet Silence

A lawyer who works hard on a case in which he believes is prone to unwarranted optimism about the chances of success. He may know full well that, for whatever reason, the tribunal is most unlikely to grant his suit, but after he has put together and submitted what appears to him as an unanswerable brief, the mirage of victory is likely to dance before his eyes. So it was with Lipson and me, and it would be idle to deny that we were disappointed by the Procuracy's response to our submission.

But surprised we were not. I doubt that any of our group ever thought it a real possibility that the Soviet authorities would acknowledge the error of their ways. After all, what had happened in these trials and in the labor camps had been done deliberately and with full awareness of its illegality. Why should they not brazen it out?

However, we had hoped that the strength of the petitions might give the Russians some misgivings about the prospect of their publication. If so, they might prefer to take some action beneficial to the prisoners, as long as we would continue to handle the cases as a straight professional matter, to be resolved by direct negotiation rather than the pressures of publicity. After all, the prisoners with whom we were concerned were insignificant numerically, and whether they stayed two or ten years in the labor camps seemed hardly a matter of moment to the Soviet State.

It was for these reasons that we had made every effort, and successfully, to keep our project out of the newspapers. Our tactics were to use the possibility rather than the fact of publicity as leverage, and thus give the Soviet authorities the benefits of face-saving. In short, while we were sure they would say no, we hoped that they might do yes—at least some yes.

Furthermore, it seemed probable that in Moscow our private demarche would not be considered by itself, but as part of the complex of issues comprising Jewish emigration in general, the Mid-East situation, and the trade negotiations with Washington. Highly placed as he was, Rudenko probably would not act on these cases without the approval of even higher authority. There was a possibility that our project might become a part of the pending Soviet-American trade and emigration negotiations, and the stronger our case was and could be made to appear, the more likely we were to reap some benefit from the situation precipitated by Senator Henry Jackson's amendment to the trade bill.

One of the reasons for the timing of the visit that Lipson and I paid to Moscow in early June was the imminence of President Nixon's visit to Moscow, expected later that month. It had seemed to us that we were more likely to reach a sympathetic ear (or any ear at all) if the Soviet officials whom we sought to engage had to bear in mind that their political superiors were about to begin important negotiations with the President of the country from which our unusual lawyers' mission had come. Whether there was any substance in these calculations, we do not know; General Rudenko did refer to the forthcoming visit of President Nixon when we saw him, but only in the context of the development of friendly relations which he said was taking place between the two governments.

After our return to the United States, we gave thought to

the possibility that the specific problems of the prisoners whose relatives we represented might be taken up in the discussions that were about to be held in Moscow between the heads of state. We were of course aware that the negotiations concerned many problems ranging over various segments of Soviet-American relations and indeed of international relations as a whole; but we had some basis for thinking that the question of emigration would figure in the list, and we thought it was time to tell the executive branch about our activity in more detail, and in other quarters, than the informational visits that had been paid to the American embassies in Israel and the Soviet Union.

Accordingly, on June 27, when the President's party was already in Russia, Eugene Gold and Leon Lipson paid a call on Leonard Garment, special counsel to the President. Garment and Gold had been friends since they were fellow students on the staff of the *Law Review* at Brooklyn Law School. Garment had not accompanied the President's party. Soviet-American affairs, and foreign policy generally, were not his primary concern. But he held a watching brief for questions of civil rights, human rights, and minority groups. Lipson has described the ensuing discussions:

> Garment received Gold and me in the executive office building. For about an hour he heard our narrative of the steps that had been taken in representing the prisoners' relatives up to that point, including of course an account of the meeting with General Rudenko a few days before. He questioned us closely on the type of procedural relief that was being requested in the papers, and certain of the cases were discussed in illustrative detail. A set of the English versions of the petitions and the memoranda of law was left with him. He told us that he would consider whether to send a message to the Presidential party in Moscow and would let us know later.
> The next day, Garment read to Gold and me the text of a message that he had drawn for the Presidential party after looking over some of the papers we had left with him. With

minor correction, the message seemed accurate and sufficiently comprehensive.

Several weeks later, Gold informed me that he had heard from Garment that the message had been sent to the Secretary of State and Helmut Sonnefeldt (the Secretary's principal adviser on Soviet affairs), and that the cases in which we were concerned had in fact been raised in the bilateral discussions. I do not know in how much detail or at what level they were discussed.

Since our turndown by the Procuracy had been expected, our period of discouragement was brief, and as yet there was no reason to lift the veil of secrecy. We would wait, and perhaps in a matter of weeks or months there would be some word or deed in Moscow that would tell us whether we had any reason to hope for ameliorative action.

It was important, however, that the Procuracy should not get the impression, while we waited, that they had seen the last of us. Shortly after I returned from my second visit to Moscow, I wrote to Rudenko, thanking him for giving me audience but pointing out that the verbal response from Malyarov hardly constituted the consideration of our petitions which he had promised.* I also told him that we would follow Malyarov's directions on clemency by asking our clients in Israel to inform their relatives in prison that they might submit petitions directly to the *praesidia*.

We did, of course, inform our clients of the meetings with Rudenko and Malyarov, and most of them sent letters to the prisoners, passing on the information. In fact, however, this course of action was not very promising, as most of the prisoners would be opposed, on conscientious grounds, to confessing a guilt they did not feel. We did not feel justified in urging that the dictates of conscience be disregarded, and it would probably have had no effect had we done so. We

---

* This letter, dated July 7, 1974, and other letters to the Procurator General, are reprinted in Appendix E, pp. 176–84.

made a few suggestions of language which some of the prisoners might find tolerable and would fulfill the formal requisites of a petition for clemency, but as far as I know none of the prisoners took the recommended step, though some of their relatives in the Soviet Union did so, without success.

Communication between the Israeli relatives and the prisoners was slow and uncertain. Many letters and parcels never reached the addresses, and often the mail was censored to the point of unintelligibility. We had no assurance, therefore, that the Procuracy's advices on clemency would ever reach the prisoners via mail from the relatives. Both for this reason and in order to jog the Procuracy again, on September 30 I wrote once more to Rudenko, asking him to forward to each of the prisoners a copy of the petition filed in his behalf and a letter from me advising him of the Procuracy's statement about clemency. Like all the other letters to Rudenko, this went unanswered.

Meanwhile, late in August, the Soviet authorities had released Silva Zalmanson. She declared that she would not leave Russia until she was able to visit with her two brothers and her husband, Kuznetsov. After allowing her a brief reunion with Kuznetsov in Moscow they insisted that she leave, and on September 10 she arrived in Israel. For a time we thought her release might be an indication of more to come, but these hopes failed to materialize, and we have found no evidence that Silva Zalmanson's release was in any way connected with our efforts. As of this writing, she is the only prisoner of conscience known to have been freed before completion of the sentence.*

As the weeks went by with no answer to my letters and no sign that our petitions were being seriously considered or having any effect, we naturally began to consider abandoning our policy of secrecy and making public disclosure of our project and its findings. What held us back during the

* But see the Postscript, p. 69.

fall of 1974 were the pending negotiations over the trade bill.

On October 19 an exchange of letters between Secretary of State Kissinger and Senator Henry Jackson was made public which indicated that the negotiations had been successful. But the Soviet authorities failed to confirm the content of these letters, and early in December they denounced the supposed undertakings on the basis of which the Kissinger-Jackson understanding had been reached.

Throughout these months of waiting, our group—generally comprising Dershowitz, Lipson, Stein, Gold, Scoppetta, Goodman, and me—had met frequently to weigh the impact of these events on our project. Even before the collapse of the Kissinger-Jackson agreement it had seemed to us increasingly improbable that our "quiet" approach to the Soviet authorities would have the results we had hoped for. There remained tactics of public disclosure and protest, which had been used with apparent success regarding the capital sentences against Dymshitz and Kuznetsov, the harassment of the Panovs, and in a few other situations. By the end of November we were all pretty well convinced that we at least had nothing to lose by such an effort and that, indeed, there was no other avenue now open to us.

However, we did not wish to change our tactics so markedly without first reporting the situation to our clients. Furthermore, during the year that had elapsed since our first visit to Israel more relatives had arrived there, as well as several prisoners who had completed their sentences. These former prisoners would be the best and freshest source of information on conditions in the labor camps, and for all these reasons it was decided that a second visit to Israel should be undertaken before publicizing the project.

8

Supplementing
the Defense Case

On Friday, December 13, I was again at the Plaza Hotel in
Tel Aviv, where I was joined two days later by my wife,
Toby Golick, a lawyer who had joined the project. Alan
Dershowitz arrived with Jeanne Baker on December 21.

I had already met with our clients, and some other prisoners' relatives who wished us to represent them. I reported on
the way the project had developed and expressed my opinion
that we had little to expect from the Soviet authorities under
present circumstances. I informed them of the conclusion
reached in New York favoring public disclosure, and invited
their views. All who spoke expressed agreement.

Our interviews during our stay in Israel fell into three
categories. There were our clients, from whom we wanted
whatever information they could give us based on their correspondence with the prisoners. There were other relatives,
some newly arrived, who wanted representation. There
were, excluding Silva Zalmanson, whom we had already met
in New York, four newly arrived former prisoners.

Our clients had little new information. Most but not all of
the prisoners had been informed of our project, but none, as
far as we could determine, had filed petitions for clemency.
On the other hand, many of their relatives, both in the Soviet
Union and in Israel, had done so. Some had been denied,

others remained unanswered. There appeared to have been no significant change in the conditions of confinement, though some individual prisoners—notably Butman and Chernoglaz—were in disciplinary troubles because of protests of one sort or another.

In consequence of our meetings with other relatives, we found ourselves with four new clients. One was Mrs. Ilana Meshener, wife of Josif Meshener from Bendery, who had been convicted together with Yakov Suslensky at Kishinev in 1970 and given a six-year sentence. According to Mrs. Meshener's affidavit, the trial was closed to the public, including the defendants' relatives, in violation of the code provisions guaranteeing the right of public trial. Otherwise, the issues were much the same as those in the second Leningrad trial, and there was the same unlawful refusal by the court to hear evidence on the nature of the allegedly anti-Soviet literature.

Alexander Feldman in Kiev and Lazar Liubarsky in Rostov were both "militant" Jews who had unsuccessfully applied for permission to emigrate, and who were making the authorities' lives miserable with letters of protest against official harassment of Jews. Their trials, both in 1973, are good examples of the concocted cases to which the Soviet authorities have resorted to silence such protesters. Feldman was given a three-and-a-half-year sentence for "malicious hooliganism" (R.S.F.S.R. Code Article 206) based on a spurious charge* of knocking a cake out of a woman's hands. Liubarsky was given four years under Articles 75 (divulging State secrets) and 190-1 (circulating false statements defaming the Soviet State). The flimsy nature of the first charge I have already described in the opening chapter; the second was based on the possession of his diary and notes which had never been intended for "circulation" (as

---

* Unofficial reports of the trial give ample reason to doubt the testimony of the supposed victim, whom the judge protected from cross-examination.

the statute requires), and his open letters of protest to the authorities.

The Pinkhasov Case

Quite different from these educated and contentious activists was the defendant in the fourth of our new cases. Pinkhas Pinkhasov was a carpenter, and had never written a letter of protest or, indeed, done anything to attract official attention except apply for permission for himself and his family to emigrate to Israel from Derbent, principal city of the Dagestan Autonomous Soviet Socialist Republic.* Apparently the Pinkhasov family was the first in that area to try to emigrate, which may account for what ensued.

In the summer of 1973 the emigration permits were issued, from the Dagestan capital, Makhachkala, and thereafter the Derbent authorities made every effort to persuade Pinkhasov to abandon his plan. He refused to be dissuaded, and on September 9, 1973, he was arrested. His wife and six children left for Israel two weeks later, but Mrs. Pinkhasov's sister and brother-in-law attended the trial in November, and then emigrated to Israel in 1974.

Pinkhasov was charged with overpricing his services as a carpenter, under Articles 92 (abuse of office) and 156 (deception of purchasers) of the R.S.F.S.R. Code. The trial was held before the Derbent City Court, which, like most Soviet trial courts, was composed of a professional judge and two "people's assessors." It so happened that one of the latter was a Jewish woman, Riya Mishayeva, who also emigrated to Israel in 1974. In this case, accordingly, we were able to confirm the relatives' account of the trial by obtaining Mishayeva's statement, embodied in affidavits attached to the petition.† Dershowitz has described the interview:

* Dagestan lies along the western coast of the Caspian Sea. The inhabitants are mostly Moslem; the region is arid and very mountainous, and many languages and dialects survive there.
† See Appendix D, pp. 168–9.

We asked to visit her and were told by the Israeli authorities that she did not want to see anybody and would probably not be cooperative since she was frightened and did not know what kind of reception she would receive in Israel after having been a Soviet lay judge and an active member of the Communist Party and of her own local trade union. We decided that notwithstanding this discouragement, we would set out to see her, no matter how unlikely it was that she would consent to talk to us. We were not able to reach her in advance, and simply drove to the south of Israel and tried to locate her home. We found out that she had moved, but after some investigation did manage to locate her. The city she was living in was one of the new Israeli development towns built especially for newly arriving Soviet immigrants. It has literally sprung up from the desert; today it consists merely of a market and several stucco four-floor and five-floor walk-up buildings, neat, clean, attractive but very spare indeed. We found Mishayeva in the apartment of some friends. The apartment itself was equipped with a kitchen table and chairs and a few mattresses and cots. The families were awaiting the shipment of their other goods from the Soviet Union. As soon as we sat down, we were offered some food—one item was a large fish wrapped in a Soviet newspaper, which led us to believe that the fish had come to Israel along with our hosts, several weeks or months before; but feeling that to reject the fish would be to insult our hosts, and being desirous of obtaining as much information as we could from the judge, we held our breaths and ate the fish, which turned out to be smoked and rather good. In any event, it was well covered by several glasses of vodka. After preliminaries, Mishayeva began to tell us in detail the story of the Pinkhasov trial. She did not seem at all reluctant to admit her own role in the case, nor to acknowledge that the Soviet authorities had virtually no evidence against Pinkhasov but were using the trial as a way to discourage him and people like him from seeking to emigrate to Israel. Mishayeva impressed us as still a convinced Communist who, for the most part, defended the Soviet system and who denied that her interest in leaving the Soviet Union stemmed in any way from her experience at that trial or at others like it.

The Derbent authorities refused to allow Pinkhasov's relatives to retain Moscow counsel and insisted that he be represented by a local attorney, Ovadya Ilyaev. None of the numerous witnesses called by the prosecution confirmed the charges. None of the witnesses requested by the defense was allowed to testify. During the trial, Judge Rasmasanov asked Mishayeva to tell Pinkhasov that the charges would be dropped if he would recall his family from Israel and remain in Derbent. When he refused, Rasmasanov and the other assessor proposed a sentence of seven years. Mishayeva, convinced of Pinkhasov's innocence, refused to sign the judgment, but did so when the other two agreed to reduce the punishment to five years, on the basis that if she refused, she would be replaced, and the seven-year sentence would be imposed. After judgment, Ilyaev refused to take an appeal, and the only other lawyer in Derbent would not touch the case. Pinkhasov himself took the appeal to the Supreme Court of the Dagestan A.S.S.R., and when that failed the case had to be dropped for lack of a lawyer, although a further appeal to the R.S.F.S.R. Supreme Court was available.

Pinkhasov, who lost a leg in an accident in 1959, was confined in a labor camp in the Kalmyck A.S.S.R.*

The Grilius Affidavits

Among the prisoners who had completed their sentences and arrived in Israel since our first visit† was Shimon Grilius

* Just before this book went to press, information was received that Pinkhasov's sentence had been reduced to two years, and that since he had already served more than his term, he had been released. See Postscript, p. 69.

† Three other newly arrived prisoners, whom we also interviewed, were Anatoly Goldfeld of the Kishinev trial, Vladimir Mogilever of the second Leningrad trial, and Valery Kukui, convicted in 1971 in Sverdlovsk under Section 190 of the R.S.F.S.R. Code. Their accounts, while interesting, added little to that of Grilius.

of the Ryazan trial, in whose behalf we had filed a petition on the request of his father and younger brother. Grilius had just been released at the expiration of a five-year sentence which he served partly in Mordovia and partly in Perm. He, like the Vudkas and Mendelevich, had been in special difficulties because of his insistence on the Jewish religious observances, and it was from him that we obtained the fullest and most up-to-date account of labor-camp conditions. His statement was then embodied in affidavits which we subsequently submitted to the Procuracy in support of the Vudka, Chernoglaz, and Mendelevich petitions.

The Grilius affidavits comprise detailed accounts of the treatment accorded those three, including the circumstances under which Yuri Vudka and Chernoglaz were transferred to the Vladimir prison. Describing the general conditions confronting the Jews in the Mordovia and Perm camps, he writes:

In both labor colonies in which I served my sentence, I and the other Jewish prisoners were subjected to abuse and persecution because we were Jews. In both camps many of the prisoners were former Nazis, including many who were Germans. The Nazis cooperated with the camp authorities and were given the best positions for work. They assisted in the camp administration, including the distribution of food and the searching and watching of the living quarters. With the knowledge of the camp administration, the Nazi prisoners often harangued the Jewish prisoners and expressed virulent anti-Semitism.

In both camps, I and the other Jewish prisoners were prevented from observing the practices of our religion. We were prevented from wearing yarmulkas, from keeping beards, from studying our religion, and from maintaining a religious diet. Jewish prayerbooks and bibles and other written documents relating solely to the Jewish religion were confiscated. Our yarmulkas were confiscated, and we were repeatedly subjected to being forcibly shaved.

In January 1973, a procurator of the Perm Oblast, named

Miakishev, came to the Perm camps and made a ruling that the Jewish prisoners would not be permitted to observe religious practices. Miakishev stated that the Declaration of Human Rights was not intended for Jews, but only for Negroes and that, although Christians were allowed to have crosses, he had received no instructions that Jews were allowed to observe their religion.

While in Israel, I had again visited the American Embassy, and informed staff members (Ambassador Keating was in the United States at the time) of the progress of our project and our intention to make it public in the near future. On the whole, we were gratified by the nature and volume of the information which this trip provided, and on our return we set about incorporating it in the petitions drafted for Meshener, Liubarsky, Feldman, and Pinkhasov, and in the affidavits of Mishayeva and Grilius.

9

Moscow: March 1975

By February 1975 the work on the four new petitions had been completed and the supporting affidavits received. In the meantime, nothing had transpired to alter our decision, reached in December, that quiet professionalism had not paid off and that there was no longer any reason to keep the project secret.

Before lifting the veil, however, we wished to make sure that the new petitions were in the hands of the Procuracy, and allow enough time to pass thereafter to allow for their review of the contents and reply, if they saw fit to make one. It would take some time to confirm delivery of the petitions by mail, and personal delivery would be preferable in case discussions were suggested.

Fortunately George Fletcher, who had returned to UCLA the previous summer, was able to make the trip. He arrived in Moscow in the evening of March 2, with the petitions and a covering letter from me to Rudenko summarizing their contents and concluding as follows:

> I assure you that it has been no part of my purpose in this matter to criticize the general system of justice in the Soviet Union, or to compare it unfavorably with the systems in other nations. In the courts of my own country there sometimes have been serious abuses and grave miscarriages of justice. It

is the obligation of lawyers everywhere to mark such flaws for the corrective attention of the judicial authorities. It was in the hope that such showings would be considered in the Soviet Union that I undertook the present representation, in the course of which I was much encouraged by the Soviet Procuracy's expressed willingness to receive and consider the petitions for review.

Regretfully, I have been forced to conclude that although the petitions have been received they have not been considered. The Procuracy's handling of the petitions submitted to you on June 12, 1974, compels the conclusion that they were denied before they were read. No responsible answer has been given to arguments and allegations which seriously impugn the integrity of the judgments rendered in these cases—a failure which must raise the inference that there are no satisfactory answers. My letters of July 7 and September 30, 1974, have gone unanswered, and information from my clients indicates that you have not transmitted to the prisoners my letters to them of September 30, 1974, written in pursuance of your suggestions with respect to clemency.

I continue to hope that you may still be persuaded to undertake a genuine review of and reasoned response to the petitions, and to take such corrective action as your high responsibilities require. If not, at least the submission of these documents will contribute to the record upon which these decisions of the Soviet courts will be judged.

When Fletcher went through customs at Sheremetov Airport, the inspector examined these documents and called his superior, and Fletcher was delayed for about forty minutes before being allowed to pass. Perhaps to compensate for the inconvenience, he was then billeted in a most luxurious penthouse duplex at the Intourist Hotel. The next day he reported his presence to the embassy, and then proceeded to the Procuracy without an appointment. The desk officer examined the documents and told him to come back the following morning. Fletcher has described his reception on March 4 at the Procuracy:

I return at about 10:45 A.M. and wait in the reception room of the Procuracy. Promptly at 11:00 A.M. I am ushered into the office of Tsibulnik. An Intourist guide is with me, but Russian does not seem to be a problem. Tsibulnik and I begin in Russian and get right down to business. He is stern, direct, and slightly nervous. He is smoking intensely. I explain my purpose of delivering the briefs and the letter. He berates me with rhetorical questions about the propriety of interfering in the Soviet legal system. I reply that I conceive of the work as a form of international legal cooperation. He questions me at length about the people involved in the project and the nature of Taylor's activities in the U.S. I explain what an American law firm is and the meaning of the letterhead on Taylor's stationery.

A secretary is present. At some point, he begins to dictate to the secretary concerning the documents received. He becomes upset by thinking that the Grilius affidavit is not mentioned in the letter to Rudenko. I point out to him that in fact it is mentioned. He questions the guide about the program arranged for me in Moscow. The innuendo seems to be that the guide should keep an eye on me. They all address me as *Georgij Nikolaevich*—a comradely form of address in Russian—and seem to enjoy the pretense that I am one of them.

At one point Tsibulnik asks us to step outside and "go for a walk," which we do. After waiting about twenty minutes in the upstairs anteroom, we are invited to return. Nothing seems to have changed. Perhaps Tsibulnik is a little more relaxed. The discussion turns to more pressing matters. Can we expect a reply? When? Would they want me to leave my telephone number in Moscow? Is there a personal message from Rudenko to Taylor? The response to these matters is that there is no desire to talk further with me ("If we need you we can contact you through Intourist"). No reply to the briefs could be expected within "a year or two." They would communicate directly with Taylor in New York. No personal message to Taylor at this time. Of course, I should tell Taylor that the Procuracy has respectfully received the briefs and the letter.

There was no further word or sign from Moscow, and no reason to delay any longer public disclosure of the project and the documents which had been produced and submitted to the Procuracy.

10

Public Disclosure:
Where We Go from Here

Since we had undertaken our project as members of the legal profession, the Association of the Bar of New York City seemed an appropriate place for its unveiling. We held a press conference there on March 18, 1975. I made a general descriptive statement, after which we answered questions from the press.

The press coverage was disappointing. I had apprised *The New York Times* in advance, and spent considerable time with the reporter assigned to the subject, but the day before the conference he was put on another assignment, and the event was covered by a different reporter. His story was given no prominence and only a few inches of space. The Columbia Broadcasting System had shown great interest; two weeks before the conference, Walter Cronkite (who as a young reporter had covered the first Nuremberg trial, and had later been a correspondent in Moscow) taped an interview with me, and the conference itself was covered by Betty Ann Bowser and a camera crew. But CBS never broadcast a foot of the many they shot. The Washington *Post,* New York *Post,* New York *Law Journal,* and a few other papers gave us more attention, as did some independent television stations and radio commentators.

Perhaps one reason for our failure to draw the amount of

notice for which we had hoped was that our prisoners were both few in number and, as individuals, comparatively obscure. Although they included some men (and after Silva Zalmanson's release they were in fact all male) of marked ability, there were no poets or ballet dancers or famous scientists—no Solzhenitsyns, Panovs, or Sakharovs. Nearly all were on the sunny side of forty, and many in their twenties, with their careers still ahead of them.

As a group, the most remarkable qualities of these prisoners is the depth of their devotion to Judaism, and the courage and intransigence with which they have persisted in their efforts to emigrate and, while still in the Soviet Union, to observe the Jewish faith. For these qualities they have paid dearly, and the price has not been lawfully exacted but oppressively extorted.

The question may well be asked whether we have more reason to expect positive results from disclosure and exposure than from the unpublicized tactics with which we carried on the project in 1974. Of course there can be no certain answer. It does appear that in some cases, such as the Panovs and the Leningrad death sentences, international outcry has had an impact on the Kremlin.

Since the initial press conference, we have endeavored to systematize the spreading of information about these cases. A degree of momentum has been achieved, to which we hope this book will contribute. It would be unfortunate if public attention remains focused exclusively on the number of Jews allowed to emigrate annually, or on personalities of international repute. Shkolnik and Pinkhasov may be untrained artisans, but the shocking injustices to which they have been subjected certainly call for denunciation just as forceful as those which have been uttered where the victims were better known.

My own opinion is that the kinds of criticism which are most likely to have an impact on Soviet policy are the comments and questions of foreign visitors, especially official and business visitors, but including general travelers as well. If it becomes apparent to the Soviet leaders that more and more of the foreigners who come there are sufficiently informed about these cases to ask questions which are difficult to answer, and which reveal a low opinion of the workings of their legal institutions, the time may come when they will decide that practices such as these cases reveal are counterproductive and bring their government into contempt.

Of course many Americans, strongly anti-Communist and hostile to the Soviet Union, will say that any idea of Soviet "justice" is a contradiction in terms, and it is altogether foolish to expect that any amends will be made. But I believe that this is a superficial view of the matter. It is true, of course, that in Communist societies law is regarded as an arm of political policy, rather than a body of principles independent of the political leadership. But despite this very different concept of the function of law, Russian lawyers are not without pride in the nature and quality of their judicial system. Perhaps our group was wrong to hope that this pride, coupled with reluctance to have these abuses exposed, would prompt corrective action. If such hopes remain unfulfilled, at least our efforts may assure the victims of these abuses that some attention has been paid to their plight, and become a part of the record on which the Soviet judicial system will be judged.

Postscript

Shortly before this book went to press, information was received, at first unverified, that the Soviet authorities had taken some kind of favorable action in the Pinkhasov case. In fact, such action had been taken in September of 1975, but apparently no official word reached Mrs. Pinkhasov in Israel until she received a letter, dated November 17, 1975, from the Moscow Municipal Advocates Collegium, signed by Kaminsky, Head of the Juridical Office, reading as follows:

> The Presidium of the Supreme Court of the Dagestanskaya Autonomous Socialist Soviet Republic has decided on the 24th of September 1975 to reduce the sentence of your husband to two years of deprivation of freedom and to release him from his place of detention following the completion of his term of punishment.
>
> As his place of detention is unknown to us at present it is therefore impossible to satisfy your request to establish contact with him.*

Since Pinkhasov had been arrested on September 9, 1973, he had already served two weeks more than two years at the time the court's action was taken. At this writ-

---

* Only an English translation of the Russian original had become available in the United States when this postscript was written.

ing, it is believed that he is in Moscow, awaiting issuance of an emigration permit.

The circumstances and considerations leading to this action are unknown to us. Others in the United States besides ourselves had taken an interest in Pinkhasov's case. The fact that one of the members of the court that sentenced him had been allowed to emigrate to Israel, and had given us a sworn statement indicating that the charges against him were concocted, is a unique feature of the situation.

Whatever the explanation, what appears to have happened is precisely what we had previously taken for a practical possibility: that is, no official admission of error, but palliative action. We continue to hope that this will not be the only example.

January 15, 1976

APPENDIXES

A. Extracts from Soviet Laws

1. CRIMINAL CODE OF THE R.S.F.S.R.

Article 15. Responsibility for Preparation of Crime and for Attempted Crime. Acquiring or arranging the means or instruments, or other intentional creation of conditions for the commission of a crime, shall be deemed preparation of a crime.

An intentional action immediately directed toward the commission of a crime shall be deemed an attempted crime, provided the crime is not brought to completion for reasons independent of the will of the guilty person.

Punishment for preparation of a crime and for attempted crime shall be assigned in accordance with the article of the Special Part of the present Code which provides for responsibility for the given crime.

In assigning punishment the court shall take into account the character and degree of social danger of the actions committed by the guilty person, the degree to which the criminal intention is carried out, and the causes by reason of which the crime is not brought to completion.

Article 17. Complicity. The intentional joint participation of two or more persons in the commission of a crime shall be deemed complicity.

Together with the perpetrators of a crime, the organizers, instigators, and accessories shall be deemed accomplices.

A person who directly commits a crime shall be deemed a perpetrator.

A person who organizes the commission of a crime or directs its commission shall be deemed an organizer.

A person who incites to the commission of a crime shall be deemed an instigator.

A person who contributes to the commission of a crime by advice, instructions, furnishing the means, or eliminating obstacles, and also a person who promises beforehand to hide the criminal, the instruments and means of committing the crime, traces of the crime, or articles criminally acquired, shall be deemed an accessory.

The degree and character of participation of each of the accomplices in the commission of a crime must be taken into account by the court in assigning punishment.

Article 43. Assignment of Milder Punishment Than That Provided by Law. If the court, taking into consideration the exceptional circumstances of a case and the personality of the guilty person, deems it necessary to assign a punishment less than the lowest limit provided by law for the given crime or to resort to another, milder type of punishment, it may permit such mitigation but shall be obliged to indicate its reasons.

Article 64. Treason. (a) Treason, that is, an act intentionally committed by a citizen of the U.S.S.R. to the detriment of the state independence, the territorial inviolability, or the military might of the U.S.S.R.: going over to the side of the enemy, espionage, transmission of a state or military secret to a foreign state, flight abroad or refusal to return from abroad to the U.S.S.R., rendering aid to a foreign state in carrying on hostile activity against the U.S.S.R., or a conspiracy for the purpose of seizing power, shall be punished by deprivation of freedom for a term of ten to fifteen years with confiscation of property with or without additional exile for a term of two to five years, or by death with confiscation of property. . . .

Article 65. Espionage. The transfer, or the stealing or collection for purpose of transfer, to a foreign state or foreign organization or its secret service, of information constituting a state or military secret, or the transfer or collection on assignment from a foreign intelligence service of any other information for use to the detriment of the interests of the U.S.S.R., if the espionage is committed by a foreigner or person without citizenship, shall be punished by deprivation of freedom for a term of seven to fifteen years with confiscation of property, with or without additional exile for a term of two to five years, or by death with confiscation of property.

Article 70. Anti-Soviet Agitation and Propaganda. Agitation or propaganda carried on for the purpose of subverting or weakening the Soviet regime or of committing particular, especially dangerous crimes against the state, or the circulation, for the same purpose, of slanderous fabrications which defame the Soviet state and social system, or the circulation or preparation or keeping, for the same purpose, of literature of such content, shall be punished by deprivation of freedom for a term of six months to seven years, with or without additional exile for a term of two to five years, or by exile for a term of two to five years.

The same actions committed by a person previously convicted of especially dangerous crimes against the state or committed in wartime shall be punished by deprivation of freedom for a term of three to ten years, with or without additional exile for a term of two to five years.

Article 72. Organizational Activity Directed to Commission of Especially Dangerous Crimes Against the State and Also Participation in Anti-Soviet Organizations. Organizational activity directed to the preparation or commission of especially dangerous crimes against the state, or to the creation of an organization which has as its purpose the commission of such crimes, or participation in an anti-Soviet organization, shall be punished in accordance with Articles 64–71 of the present Code.

Article 75. Divulgence of State Secret. Divulgence of information constituting a state secret by a person to whom such information has been entrusted or has become known because of his position or work, in the absence of the indicia of treason or espionage, shall be punished by deprivation of freedom for a term of two to five years.

The same act, if it results in serious consequences, shall be punished by deprivation of freedom for a term of five to eight years.

Article 83. Illegal Exit Abroad and Illegal Entry Into the U.S.S.R. Exit abroad, entry into the U.S.S.R., or crossing the border without the requisite passport or the permission of the proper authorities, shall be punished by deprivation of freedom for a term of one to three years.

Operation of the present article shall not extend to instances of arrival in the U.S.S.R. of foreign citizens, without the requisite passport or permit, for exercise of the right of asylum granted by the Constitution of the U.S.S.R.

Article 88–1. Failure to Report Crimes Against the State. The failure to report crimes against the state that are known to be in preparation or to have been committed, provided for by Articles 64 (treason), 65 (espionage), 66 and 67 (terrorist act), 68 (sabotage), 69 (wrecking), 72 (organizational activity directed at commission of especially dangerous crimes against the state and also participation in anti-Soviet organizations), 77 (banditry), 87 (making or passing of counterfeit money or securities) of the present Code, shall be punished by deprivation of freedom for a term of one to three years or by correctional tasks for a term of six months to one year.

Article 92. Stealing of State or Social Property, Committed by Appropriation or Embezzlement or by Abuse of Official Position. The appropriation or embezzlement of state or social property which has been entrusted to the guilty person, or the taking possession of state or social property for a mercenary purpose through abuse by an official of his office, shall be punished by deprivation of freedom for a term not exceeding four years, or by correctional tasks for a term not exceeding one year, or by deprivation of the right to occupy specified offices or to engage in specified activity.

The same actions committed repeatedly or by a group of persons in accordance with a preliminary agreement shall be punished by deprivation of freedom for a term not exceeding seven years with or without deprivation of the right to occupy specified offices or to engage in specified activity.

Actions provided for by paragraphs one or two of the present article, which have caused serious loss to the state or to a social organization, shall be punished by deprivation of freedom for a term of six to fifteen years with or without confiscation of property and by deprivation of the right to occupy specified offices or to engage in specified activity.

Article 93–1. Stealing of State or Social Property on an Especially Large Scale. The stealing of state or social property on an especially large scale, regardless of the manner of stealing (Articles 89–93), shall be punished by deprivation of freedom for a term of eight to fifteen years with confiscation of property, with or without exile, or by death with confiscation of property.

Article 143. Obstruction of Performance of Religious Rites. The obstruction of the performance of religious rites, insofar as they do not violate public order and are not accompanied by infringement of the rights of citizens, shall be punished by correctional tasks for a term not exceeding six months or by social censure.

Article 156. Deception of Purchasers. False measuring, false weighing, marking up of established retail prices, false reckoning, or any other deception of purchasers in stores or any other trade enterprises or in public eating establishments shall be punished by deprivation of freedom for a term not exceeding two years, or by correctional tasks for a term not exceeding one year, or by deprivation of the right to occupy offices in trade enterprises or public eating establishments.

The same actions committed in accordance with a preliminary agreement of a group of persons, or on a large scale, or by persons previously convicted of the same crimes shall be punished by deprivation of freedom for a term of two to seven years with or without confiscation of property, with deprivation of the right to occupy offices in trade enterprises or public eating establishments.

Article 190. Failure to Report Crimes. The failure to report known crimes which are being prepared or have been committed, provided for by Articles 102, 103, and 240, subsection "c" (intentional homicide), 117, paragraphs two and three (rape under aggravating circumstances), 89, paragraph three, and 144, paragraph three (theft under aggravating circumstances), 90, paragraph three, and 145, paragraph three (open stealing under aggravating circumstances), 91 and 146 (assault with intent to rob), 92, paragraph three (stealing state or social property, committed by appropriation, embezzlement, or abuse of official position, under aggravating circumstances), 93, paragraph three, and 147, paragraph three (swindling under aggravating circumstances), 93–1 (stealing state or social property on especially large scale), 173, paragraph two, 174, paragraph two, and 174–1, paragraph two (taking or giving a bribe or acting as an intermediary in bribery under aggravating circumstances), 191–2 (infringing the life of a policeman or people's guard), 218–1, paragraphs two and three (stealing of a firearm, ammunition, or explosives) of the present Code shall be punished by deprivation of freedom for a term not exceeding three years or by correctional tasks for a term not exceeding one year.

Article 190–1. Circulation of Fabrications Known to Be False Which Defame Soviet State and Social System. The systematic circulation in an oral form of fabrications known to be false which defame the Soviet state and social system and, likewise, the preparation or circulation in written, printed, or any other form of works of such content shall be punished by deprivation of freedom for a term not exceeding three years, or by correctional tasks for a term not exceeding one year, or by a fine not exceeding one hundred rubles.

Article 206. Hooliganism. Hooliganism, that is, intentional actions violating public order in a coarse manner and expressing a clear disrespect toward society, and, likewise, petty hooliganism committed by a person to whom a measure of administrative pressure for petty hooliganism has been applied within a year, shall be punished by deprivation of freedom for a term of six months to one year, or by correctional tasks for the same term, or by a fine of thirty to fifty rubles.

Malicious hooliganism, that is, the same actions distinguished in their content by exceptional cynicism or special impudence, or connected with resisting a representative of authority or representative of the public fulfilling duties for protection of public order or other citizens who are restraining hooliganistic actions and, likewise, actions which are committed by a person previously convicted of hooliganism, shall be punished by deprivation of freedom for a term of one to five years.

Actions provided for by paragraphs one or two of the present article, if committed with the use or attempted use of a firearm, a knife, brass knuckles, other sidearms, or any other objects especially adapted to the infliction of bodily injuries, shall be punished by deprivation of freedom for a term of three to seven years.

Article 212–1. Driving Away Means of Motor Transport. The driving away of means of motor transport or other self-propelled vehicles without the purpose of stealing them shall be punished by deprivation of freedom for a term not exceeding one year, or by correctional tasks for the same period, or by a fine not exceeding one hundred rubles, or shall entail application of measures of social pressure.

The same actions committed a second time shall be punished by deprivation of freedom for a term not exceeding three years or by correctional tasks for a term not exceeding one year.

2. Code of Criminal Procedure of the R.S.F.S.R.

Article 5. Circumstances Precluding Criminal Proceedings. A criminal case may not be initiated, and if initiated shall be subject to termination: . . . (10) with respect to a person concerning whom under the same accusation there is an unrevoked decree of an agency of inquiry, of an investigator, or of a procurator to terminate the case, except in instances provided by Articles 255 and 256 of the present Code.

Article 19. Securing to an Accused the Right to Defense. An accused shall have the right to defense. A court, procurator, investigator, and person conducting an inquiry shall be obliged to secure to the accused the possibility of defending himself against the accusation brought against him by the means and methods established by law, and to secure protection of his personal and property rights.

Article 20. Thorough, Complete, and Objective Analysis of Circumstances of Case. A court, procurator, investigator, and person conducting an inquiry shall be obliged to take all measures provided by law for a thorough, complete, and objective analysis of the circumstances of the case, and to expose circumstances tending both to convict and to acquit the accused, as well as those tending to aggravate and to mitigate his guilt.

The court, procurator, investigator, and person conducting the inquiry shall not have the right to shift the obligation of proof to the accused.

It shall be prohibited to solicit the accused's testimony by force, threats, or any other illegal measures.

Article 43. Transfer of Criminal Case to Another Jurisdiction. A judge or a court in administrative session, having established that a case which has been accepted is not within the jurisdiction of the given court, shall refer the case to another jurisdiction.

A court, having established that a case it is conducting is within the jurisdiction of another similar court, shall have the right to continue to conduct the case only in the event that it has already commenced to consider it in judicial session. If, however, a case is within the jurisdiction of a higher court or a military tribunal, it shall in all instances be subject to referral to the jurisdiction of such higher court or military tribunal.

It shall not be permitted to transfer to a lower court a case whose consideration in judicial session of a higher court has commenced.

Article 46. The Accused. A person with respect to whom, in accordance with the procedure established by the present Code, a decree to prosecute as the accused has been rendered, shall be deemed the accused.

An accused who is brought to trial shall be called a person brought to trial; an accused with respect to whom a judgment of conviction has been rendered shall be called a convicted person.

The accused shall have the right to know what he is accused of and to give explanations concerning the accusation presented to him; to present evidence; to submit petitions; to become acquainted with all the materials of the case upon completion of the preliminary investigation or inquiry; to have defense counsel from the moment provided for by Article 47 of the present Code; to participate in the judicial examination in the court of first instance; to submit challenges; and to appeal from the actions and decisions of the person conducting the inquiry, the investigator, procurator, and court.

The person brought to trial shall have the right to the last word.

*Article 47. Participation of Defense Counsel in Criminal Pro-

* Article 47 is revised by the Edicts of the Presidium of the Supreme Soviet of the U.S.S.R. of August 31, 1970 (*Vedomosti S.S.S.R.*, September 9, 1970, no. 36, item 362) and of February 3, 1972 (*Vedomosti S.S.S.R.,* February 9, 1972, no. 6, item 51) amending Article 22 of the Fundamental Principles of Criminal Procedure of the U.S.S.R. and the Union Republics. The amended Article 22 is set forth below with the changes italicized for the reader's convenience. As of March 1, 1972, the R.S.F.S.R. Code of Criminal Procedure had not been amended to conform to the U.S.S.R. edicts.

Article 22. *Participation of defense counsel in criminal proceedings.* Defense counsel shall be permitted to participate in a case from the moment the accused is informed of the completion of the preliminary investigation and is presented with all the proceedings of the case to become acquainted with them. *By decree of the procurator, defense counsel may be permitted to participate in the case from the moment the accusation is presented.*

Participation of defense counsel in the preliminary investigation and at the judicial examination shall be obligatory in cases of minors, of *deaf, dumb, and blind persons,* and of other persons who by reason of their physical or psychological defects cannot themselves exercise their right to defense. *In these situations the defense counsel shall be allowed to participate in the case from the moment of the presentation of the accusation.*

In cases of persons who do not have command of the language in which the proceedings are conducted and also of persons accused of committing crimes for which the death penalty may be imposed as a measure of

ceedings. Defense counsel shall be permitted to participate in a case from the moment the accused is informed of the completion of the preliminary investigation and is presented with all the proceedings of the case to become acquainted with them.

In cases of crimes of minors, as well as of persons who by reason of their physical or mental defects are not themselves able to exercise their right to defense, defense counsel shall be permitted to participate in the case from the moment the accusation is presented.

In cases in which a preliminary investigation is not conducted, defense counsel shall be permitted from the moment the accused is brought to trial.

Advocates and representatives of trade unions and of other social organizations shall be permitted to serve as defense counsel.

By ruling of the court or decree of the judge, near relatives and legal representatives of the accused, as well as other persons, shall be permitted to serve as defense counsel.

The same person may not be defense counsel for two accused persons if the interests of one of them conflict with the interests of the other.

Article 50. Refusal of Defense Counsel. The accused shall have the right at any moment in the conduct of a case to refuse defense counsel. Such a refusal shall be permitted only upon the initiative of the accused himself and may not be an obstacle to the continued participation in the case of the state or social accuser or of defense counsel for other persons brought to trial.

A petition to refuse defense counsel by a minor or by an accused who by reason of his physical or mental defects is not himself able to exercise his right to defense shall not be binding on the court, investigator, or procurator, respectively.

Article 51. Duties and Rights of Defense Counsel. Defense counsel shall be obliged to make use of all means and methods of defense indicated in the law for the purpose of explaining the circumstances tending to acquit the accused or to mitigate his responsibility, and to render the accused necessary legal aid.

From the moment he is permitted to participate in a case defense counsel shall have the right to meet with the accused; to become acquainted with all the materials of the case and to copy necessary

---

punishment, the participation of defense counsel is obligatory from the moment the accused is informed of the completion of the preliminary investigation and is presented with all the proceedings of the case to become acquainted with them.

Obligatory participation of defense counsel in a case may also take place in other instances defined by legislation of union republics.

Advocates, representatives of trade unions and of other social organizations, and other persons to whom such right is given by legislation of union republics shall be permitted to serve as defense counsel.

information therefrom; to present evidence; to submit petitions; to participate in the judicial examination; to submit challenges; to appeal from actions and decisions of the investigator, procurator, and court. With the permission of the investigator, defense counsel may be present during interrogations of the accused and during the conduct of any other investigative actions performed upon petition of the accused or of his defense counsel.

In instances where defense counsel is permitted to participate in a case from the moment the accusation is presented he may, in addition:

1. be present at the presentation of the accusation and the interrogation of the accused and, with the permission of the investigator, put questions to the accused;

2. be present when other investigative actions are carried out and, with the permission of the investigator, put questions to witnesses, victims, and experts;

3. make written remarks in connection with the correctness and completeness of the entries in the record of an investigative action in which he has participated.

An investigator may exclude questions of the defense counsel, but shall be obliged to enter the excluded questions in the record.

An advocate shall not have the right to withdraw from the defense of an accused after he has accepted it.

Article 68. Circumstances Subject to Proof in Criminal Case. In an inquiry or preliminary investigation and in the examination of a criminal case in court the following shall be subject to proof:

1. the occurrence of the crime (time, place, method, and other circumstances of the commission of the crime);

2. the guilt of the accused in committing the crime and motives for the crime;

3. circumstances stated in Articles 38 and 39 of the R.S.F.S.R. Criminal Code which influence the degree and character of the responsibility of the accused, as well as other circumstances characterizing the personality of the accused;

4. the character and extent of loss caused by the crime.

Circumstances that have facilitated the commission of the crime shall also be subject to ascertainment.

Article 78. Expert Examination. An expert examination shall be assigned in instances when, in the conduct of the inquiry or preliminary investigation or during the judicial examination, special knowledge of science, engineering, art, or a trade is necessary. An expert examination shall be carried out by experts of appropriate institutions or by other specialists assigned by a person conducting an inquiry, investigator, procurator, or court. Any person possessing knowledge necessary for giving an opinion may be summoned as an expert.

The request of the person conducting an inquiry, investigator, procurator, or court that an expert be summoned shall be binding on the manager of the institution, enterprise, or organization where the expert works. The questions put to the expert and his opinion may not go beyond the limits of the special knowledge of the expert.

Article 84. Preserving Real Evidence. Real evidence must be described in detail in the records of a view, photographed if possible, and attached to the file of the case, by special decree of a person conducting an inquiry, investigator or procurator, or by ruling of a court. Real evidence must be preserved with the file of the criminal case.

If certain articles because of their bulk or for other reasons cannot be preserved with the file of a criminal case, they must be photographed and, if possible, sealed and preserved in a place indicated by the person conducting the inquiry, investigator, procurator, or court, and there must be an appropriate certificate thereof in the file of the case.

When a case is transferred from an agency of inquiry to an investigator or from one agency of inquiry or investigator to another, and also when a case is referred to a procurator or court or when a case is transferred from one court to another, real evidence shall be forwarded with the file of the case, except in the instance provided for by paragraph two of the present article.

Article 184. Procedure for Assignment of Expert Examination. If an investigator deems an expert examination to be necessary, he shall draw up a decree to such effect, which shall indicate the grounds for assigning an expert examination, the surname of the expert or name of the institution at which the expert examination must be conducted, the questions placed before the expert, and the materials made available to the expert.

Before appointing an expert, the investigator shall ascertain the necessary data about his specialty and competence.

The investigator shall be obliged to acquaint the accused with the decree assigning expert examination and to explain his rights as established by Article 185 of the present Code. A record thereof shall be drawn up, and signed by the investigator and the accused.

The decree to assign a forensic psychiatric expert examination and the opinion of the experts shall not be announced to the accused if his mental state makes this impossible.

Article 185. Rights of Accused During Assignment and Conduct of Expert Examination. During the assignment and conduct of an expert examination an accused shall have the right to:

1. challenge the expert;
2. request the assignment of an expert from among persons indicated by him;
3. present additional questions in order to obtain the opinion of an expert concerning them;
4. be present, with the permission of the investigator, at the expert examination and give explanations to the expert;
5. become acquainted with the opinion of the expert.

In the event that he grants a petition of the accused, the investigator shall accordingly change or add to his decree to assign an expert examination.

In the event that he denies a petition, the investigator shall render a decree which shall be announced to the accused, and a receipt obtained from him.

Article 202. Rights of Defense Counsel in Becoming Acquainted With All Materials of Case. An accused's defense counsel shall have the right:

1. to meet with the accused alone;
2. to acquaint himself with all the materials of the case and to copy necessary information therefrom;
3. to discuss with the accused the question of filing petitions;
4. to file petitions with respect to the conduct of investigative actions, the obtaining of evidence and having it attached to the file of the case, and all other questions of significance for the case;
5. to file a challenge of an investigator, procurator, expert, specialist, or interpreter;
6. to bring complaints to the procurator against actions of the investigator which violate or prejudice the rights of defense counsel or of the accused;
7. to be present, with the permission of the investigator, during investigative actions performed in accordance with petitions filed by the accused and his defense counsel.

Article 232. Returning Case for Supplementary Investigation. A court in administrative session shall refer a case for supplementary investigation in the event of:

1. an insufficiency in the conduct of the inquiry or preliminary investigation;
2. the substantial violation of criminal procedure law in the conduct of the inquiry or preliminary investigation;
3. the existence of grounds for the presentation to the accused of another accusation connected with the one previously presented, or for changing the accusation to a graver one or one

differing substantially in factual circumstances from the accusation contained in the conclusion to indict;

4. the existence of grounds for instituting criminal proceedings against other persons in the given case when it is impossible to separate the materials of the case concerning them;

5. incorrect joinder or disjoinder of a case.

A case shall be referred to the procurator for supplementary investigation. In this connection the court shall be obliged to indicate in its ruling upon what grounds the case is returned and what circumstances must be elucidated supplementarily.

When referring a case for supplementary investigation, a court shall be obliged to resolve the question of a measure of restraint with respect to the accused.

Article 240. Directness, Oral Nature, and Continuity of Judicial Examination. In considering a case, a court of first instance shall be obliged to analyze the evidence in the case directly: to interrogate persons brought to trial, victims, and witnesses, hear opinions of experts, view real evidence, and publicly disclose records and other documents.

The judicial session for each case shall proceed continuously except for time designated for rest. Consideration of other cases by the same judges before completion of the hearing of a case already commenced shall not be permitted.

Article 245. Equality of Rights of Participants in Judicial Examination. An accuser, person brought to trial, and defense counsel, as well as a victim, civil plaintiff, civil defendant, and their representatives at a judicial examination shall enjoy equal rights in presenting evidence, participating in the analysis of the evidence, and submitting petitions.

Article 246. Participation of Person Brought to Trial in Judicial Examination. The examination of a case in a session of a court of first instance shall proceed with the participation of the person brought to trial, whose appearance in court shall be obligatory.

The examination of a case in the absence of the person brought to trial may be permitted only in exceptional instances, if this does not obstruct the establishment of the truth in the case:

1. when the person brought to trial is outside the U.S.S.R. and evades appearance in court;

2. when, in a case of a crime for which the punishment of deprivation of freedom may not be assigned, the person brought to trial petitions for examination of the case in his absence. A court shall have the right, however, to deem the appearance of the person brought to trial obligatory.

Article 249. Participation of Defense Counsel in Judicial Examination. A defense counsel shall take part in the analysis of the evidence, shall express his opinion on questions arising during the judicial examination, shall set forth to the court the views of the defense on the substance of the accusation relating to circumstances tending to mitigate responsibility and concerning the measure of punishment and civil-law consequences of the crime.

Article 255. Initiating of Criminal Case Upon New Accusation. If a judicial examination establishes circumstances indicating that a person brought to trial has committed a crime for which no accusation has been previously presented to him, the court shall, without suspending examination, initiate a case upon a new accusation and shall refer the necessary materials for inquiry or preliminary investigation in the usual manner.

In the event that the new accusation is connected with the original one and their separate consideration is not possible, the whole case must be returned for supplementary investigation.

Article 276. Filing and Disposition of Petitions. The person presiding shall ask the accuser, person brought to trial, and his defense counsel, as well as the victim, civil plaintiff, civil defendant, or their representatives, whether they have petitions to summon new witnesses, experts, and specialists or to acquire real evidence and documents. A person who has submitted a petition is obliged to indicate for the establishment of exactly what circumstances any supplementary evidence is necessary.

Having heard the opinion of the remaining participants in the judicial examination, the court must discuss each petition filed, must grant it if the circumstances subject to elucidation are of significance for the case, or render a reasoned ruling refusing to grant the petition.

The refusal of the court to grant a petition shall not limit the right of the person whose petition has been refused to file it in the future depending on the course of the judicial examination.

The court shall have the right, regardless of whether a petition has been filed, to render a ruling to summon new witnesses, assign an expert examination, or acquire documents and other evidence.

Article 283. Interrogation of Witnesses. Witnesses shall be interrogated separately and in the absence of witnesses not yet interrogated.

The person presiding shall ascertain the relationships among a witness and the person brought to trial and victim and shall propose to the witness that he communicate everything that is known to him in the case. Thereafter the judges and accusers, as well as the victim, the civil plaintiff, the civil defendant, and their representatives, defense counsel, and the persons brought to trial shall interrogate the witness. If a witness has been summoned to the judicial session upon a petition of one of the participants of the judicial examination, such participant shall put questions to such witness first. The person presiding shall eliminate questions having no relation to the case.

Judges shall have the right to put questions to a witness at any moment of the judicial investigation.

Witnesses who have been interrogated shall remain in the courtroom and may not withdraw before the completion of the judicial investigation without the permission of the court.

The person presiding may allow witnesses who have been interrogated to withdraw from the courtroom earlier than the completion of the judicial investigation only upon hearing the opinions of the accuser, person brought to trial, and defense counsel as well as of the victim, civil plaintiff, civil defendant, and their representatives.

Article 301. Legality and Well-Founded Nature of Judgment. A judgment of a court must be legal and well-founded.

The court shall found the judgment only on evidence which has been considered at the judicial session.

The judgment of the court must be reasoned.

Article 303. Questions Resolved by Court When Decreeing Judgment. When decreeing judgment a court shall resolve the following questions in the conference room:

1. whether the act which the person brought to trial is accused of committing has taken place;

2. whether such act contains the elements of a crime and exactly which criminal law provides for it;

3. whether the person brought to trial has committed such act;

4. whether the person brought to trial is guilty of committing such crime;

5. whether the person brought to trial is subject to punishment for the crime committed by him;

6. exactly which punishment must be assigned to the person brought to trial and whether it is subject to being served by the person brought to trial;

6–1. whether there are grounds for deeming the person brought to trial an especially dangerous recidivist; which type of correctional labor institution with the corresponding regimen must be determined for the person brought to trial in assigning him the punishment of deprivation of freedom;

7. whether the civil suit is subject to satisfaction, in whose favor, and to what extent, and also, if a civil suit has not been brought, whether the material loss is subject to compensation;

8. how to deal with the real evidence;

9. on whom and in what amount court costs must be imposed;

10. the measure of restraint with respect to the person brought to trial.

If the person brought to trial is accused of committing several crimes, the court shall resolve for each crime separately the questions indicated in subsections 1–6 of the present article.

If several persons brought to trial are accused of committing a crime, the court shall resolve these questions separately with respect to each person brought to trial.

Article 309. Types of Judgments. A judgment of a court may be either of conviction or acquittal.

A judgment of conviction may not be founded on assumptions and shall be decreed only if during the course of the judicial examination the guilt of the person brought to trial in committing the crime is proved. The court shall decree a judgment of conviction without assigning punishment if, by the time the case is considered in court, the act has lost its social danger or the person who has committed it has ceased to be socially dangerous.

A judgment of acquittal shall be decreed in instances when:

1. the event of a crime is not established;

2. the act of the person brought to trial does not contain the elements of a crime;

3. participation of the person brought to trial in the commission of the crime is not proved.

If, in decreeing a judgment of acquittal, because of lack of proof of the participation of the person brought to trial in the commission of the crime, the person who committed such crime remains undisclosed, the court shall, after the decree has taken legal effect, refer the case to the procurator to take measures to establish the person subject to prosecution as the accused.

Article 314. Descriptive Part of Judgment. The descriptive part of a judgment of conviction must contain a description of the criminal act deemed proved, with an indication of the place, time, and method of its commission and the nature of the guilt, motives, and consequences of the crime; the evidence on which the court's conclusions are founded and the reasons for which the court has rejected other evidence; indications of circumstances tending to mitigate or aggravate responsibility; and in the event that part of the accusation is deemed unfounded, the grounds therefor; the court shall also be obliged to adduce the reasons for deeming the person brought to trial an especially dangerous recidivist, for changing the accusation, if such has been done in court, and, when necessary, the reasons relating to the measure of punishment selected. Reasons must be given, in addition, for the relief of the person brought to trial from punishment, the application of conditional conviction, as well as for the assignment of punishment lower than the lowest limit provided by the criminal law for the given crime, resort to another milder punishment, or the assignment of a type of correctional labor colony or educational labor colony with deviation from the general rules. If there is more than one person brought to trial in the case, the enumerated indications must be made with respect to each of the persons brought to trial individually.

The descriptive part of a judgment of acquittal shall set forth the substance of the accusation upon which the accused has been brought to trial; the circumstances of the case established by the court; it shall adduce the evidence serving as the basis for acquitting the person brought to trial, with an indication of the reasons explaining why the court rejects the evidence on which the accusation has been founded. Inclusion in a judgment of acquittal of formulations that cast doubt on the innocence of the acquitted person shall not be permitted.

The descriptive part of a judgment of conviction or acquittal must contain the reasons underlying the decision of the court with respect to the civil suit or compensation of the material loss caused by the crime.

Article 342. Grounds for Vacating or Changing Judgment. The grounds for vacating or changing a judgment in the consideration of a case by way of cassation are:

1. one-sidedness or incompleteness of the inquiry or of the preliminary or judicial investigation;

2. lack of correspondence of the court's findings, set forth in the judgment, with the factual circumstances of the case;

3. substantial violation of the criminal procedure law;

4. incorrect application of the criminal law;

5. lack of correspondence of the punishment assigned by the court with the gravity of the crime or the personality of the convicted person.

Article 362. Relief From Serving Punishment Because of Illness. In the event that, while serving punishment, a sentenced person has contracted a chronic mental or other grave illness preventing serving the punishment, the court shall have the right, upon the proposal of the director of the agency conducting the execution of the punishment based on the opinion of a doctors' commission, to render a ruling to relieve him from further serving of the punishment.

When relieving from further serving of punishment a convicted person who has contracted a chronic mental illness, the court shall have the right to apply compulsory measures of a medical character or to transfer him to the care of agencies of public health.

When deciding the question of relieving from further serving of punishment persons who have contracted a grave illness other than persons who have contracted a mental illness, the court shall take into account the gravity of the crime committed, the personality of the convicted person, and other circumstances.

Article 365. Replacing Correctional Tasks and Fine by Other Measures of Punishment. Replacement of correctional tasks by a fine, social censure, or imposition of the duty to make amends for harm caused, with respect to persons deemed incapable of working and in accordance with Article 27 of the R.S.F.S.R. Criminal Code, as well as replacement of correctional tasks by deprivation of freedom in accordance with Article 28 of the R.S.F.S.R. Criminal Code, shall be carried out by a court upon the proposal of the agency executing that type of punishment.

Replacement of a fine by correctional tasks shall be carried out by a court in accordance with Article 30 of the R.S.F.S.R. Criminal Code.

Article 371. Review by Way of Judicial Supervision of Judgment, Ruling, or Decree of Court Which Has Taken Legal Effect. The review by way of judicial supervision of a judgment, ruling, or decree of a court which has taken legal effect shall be permitted only on protest of a procurator or a chairman of a court or their deputies, as designated in the present article.

The following shall have the right to bring protests:

1. the U.S.S.R. Procurator General—of judgments, rulings, and decrees of any court of the R.S.F.S.R.;

2. the President of the U.S.S.R. Supreme Court—of decrees of the Presidium as well as of judgments and rulings of the Judicial Division for Criminal Cases of the R.S.F.S.R. Supreme Court, acting as a court of first instance;

3. U.S.S.R. Deputy Procurators General—of judgments, rulings, and decrees of any court of the R.S.F.S.R. with the exception of decrees of the Presidium of the R.S.F.S.R. Supreme Court;

4. Deputy Presidents of the U.S.S.R. Supreme Court—of judgments and rulings of the Judicial Division for Criminal Cases of the R.S.F.S.R. Supreme Court, acting as a court of first instance;

5. the R.S.F.S.R. Procurator and President of the R.S.F.S.R. Supreme Court and their deputies—of judgments, rulings, and decrees of any court in the R.S.F.S.R. with the exception of decrees of the Presidium of the R.S.F.S.R. Supreme Court.

6. the president of the supreme court of an autonomous republic, territorial, regional, or city court, court of an autonomous region, or court of a national area, procurator of an autonomous republic, territory, region, autonomous region, or national area—of a judgment or ruling of a district (city) people's court or a ruling of a judicial division for criminal cases of the supreme court of the autonomous republic, territorial, regional, or city court, court of an autonomous region, or court of a national area, respectively, which has considered the case by way of cassation.

Protests of judgments of military tribunals shall be brought in accordance with the procedure established by Articles 20 and 21 of the Statute on Military Tribunals.

A person who has brought a protest shall have the right to withdraw it. A protest brought by a procurator may be withdrawn by a higher procurator. Withdrawal of a protest shall be permitted only before the commencement of the judicial session during which the protest is subject to consideration.

Article 379. Grounds for Vacating or Changing Judgment, Ruling, or Decree of Court Which Has Taken Legal Effect. The circumstances stated in Article 342 of the present Code shall constitute the grounds for vacating or changing a judgment in the consideration of a case by way of judicial supervision.

Rulings of a court of first instance, decrees of a judge, rulings of the cassational instance, and rulings and decrees of the supervisory instance shall be subject to being vacated or changed if the court considering the protest deems that by such ruling or decree the court of first instance has rendered an illegal or unfounded decision, or that a higher court has without basis left unchanged, vacated, or changed previous rulings, decrees, or the judgment in the case, or that in the consideration of the case in the higher court violations of the law have been permitted which have affected or might have affected the correctness of the ruling or decree rendered by it.

3. CONSTITUTION OF THE U.S.S.R.

Article 111. Examination of cases in all courts of the U.S.S.R. shall be open, insofar as exceptions are not provided by law, with the accused being guaranteed the right to defense.

Article 123. Equality of rights of citizens of the U.S.S.R., regardless of their nationality or race, in all spheres of economic, state, cultural, and social-political life shall be an indefeasible law.

Any kind of direct or indirect restriction of rights or, conversely, establishment of direct or indirect privileges of citizens on account of their race or nationality, and also any advocacy of racial or national exclusiveness or of hatred or contempt, shall be punished by law.

Article 124. In order to guarantee to citizens freedom of conscience, the church in the U.S.S.R. shall be separated from the state, and the school from the church. Freedom of religious worship and freedom of anti-religious propaganda shall be recognized for all citizens.

Article 129. The U.S.S.R. shall afford the right of asylum to foreign citizens persecuted for defending the interests of the working people, for their scholarly activities, or for their struggle for national liberation.

4. CONSTITUTION OF THE R.S.F.S.R.

Article 127. Equality of rights of citizens of the R.S.F.S.R., regardless of their nationality or race, in all spheres of economic, state, cultural, and social-political life shall be an indefeasible law.

Any kind of direct or indirect restriction of rights, or, conversely, establishment of direct or indirect privileges of citizens on account of their race or nationality, and also any advocacy of racial or national exclusiveness or of hatred or contempt, shall be punished by law.

Article 128. In order to guarantee to citizens freedom of conscience, the church in the R.S.F.S.R. shall be separated from the state, and the school from the church. Freedom of religious worship and freedom of anti-religious propaganda shall be recognized for all citizens.

5. STATUTE ON THE PROCURACY

Article 22. The Procurator General of the U.S.S.R. and procurators subordinate to him shall be obliged to exercise supervision over the legality and grounds for judgments, decisions, rulings, and decrees rendered by judicial agencies.

Article 23. The Procurator General of the U.S.S.R. and procurators subordinate to him shall:

1. participate in administrative sessions of a court;
2. participate in consideration of criminal and civil cases in judicial sessions and give conclusions on questions arising during judicial consideration;
3. support the state accusation in court during consideration of criminal cases;

4. present claims [by instituting] either civil cases or civil suits in criminal cases, and support the suits in court, if such is required for protection of state or social interests or of the rights or legal interests of citizens;

5. lodge protests, in the procedure established by law, against illegal or unjustified judgments, decisions, rulings, or decrees of judicial agencies;

6. give conclusions with respect to criminal and civil cases being considered by a higher court on appeal or on protest;

7. exercise supervision over execution of judgments of a court.

Article 25. The right of lodging protests against judgments, decisions, rulings, and decrees of a court which have taken legal effect shall belong:

to the Procurator General of the U.S.S.R. and his deputies, with respect to judgments, decisions, rulings, and decrees of any court of the U.S.S.R. or of union or autonomous republics;

to the procurator of a union republic and his deputies, with respect to judgments, decisions, rulings, and decrees of courts of the union republic and of autonomous republics forming part of it, except for decrees of the Presidium of the Supreme Court of the union republic;

to the procurator of an autonomous republic, with respect to judgments, decisions, and rulings of people's courts of the autonomous republic, as well as the rulings of judicial divisions of the Supreme Court of the autonomous republic as a court of second instance;

to the procurator of a territory, region, or autonomous region, with respect to judgments, decisions, and rulings of people's courts, as well as rulings of judicial divisions of the territorial or regional court, or court of the autonomous region, respectively, as a court of second instance;

to the Chief Military Procurator, with respect to judgments and rulings of any military tribunal;

to the military procurator of a military area (or fleet), with respect to judgments and rulings of inferior military tribunals.

Article 32. The Procurator General of the U.S.S.R. and procurators subordinate to him, within the limits of their competence, shall be obliged to exercise supervision to the end that only persons confined under guard with the sanction of a procurator or by decree of a court should be kept in places of deprivation of freedom, as well as [supervision] over observance of the rules established by law for the keeping of confined persons.

Agencies of the procuracy shall be charged with responsibility for observance of socialist legality in places of deprivation of freedom.

Article 33. A procurator shall be obliged to visit regularly places of deprivation of freedom to familiarize himself at first hand with the operation of their administration, to suspend execution of orders or regulations of the administration of places of deprivation of freedom which contradict the law and to protest them in the established procedure, as well as to take measures to bring to criminal or disciplinary responsibility persons guilty of violation of legality in places of deprivation of freedom.

Article 34. A procurator shall be obliged to free from under guard, without delay, anyone who has been unlawfully subjected to arrest or unlawfully kept under guard in places of deprivation of freedom.

Article 35. In exercising supervision over the legality of the keeping of persons confined in places of deprivation of freedom, the Procurator General of the U.S.S.R. and procurators subordinate to him, within the limits of their competence, shall have the right:

1. with the aim of verifying observance of the procedure established by law for the keeping of persons confined under guard, to visit places of deprivation of freedom at any time, with unobstructed access to all buildings;

2. to familiarize himself with documents on the basis of which persons have been subjected to deprivation of freedom;

3. personally to question confined persons;

4. to verify conformity to law of orders and regulations of the administration of places of deprivation of freedom which determine the conditions and regime for the keeping of confined persons;

5. to require personal explanations of representatives of the administration of places of deprivation of freedom concerning violations of the legality of keeping of confined persons.

Article 36. The administration of a place of deprivation of freedom shall be obliged within twenty-four hours to send to a procurator a complaint addressed to him or a petition of a confined person.

A procurator who has received a complaint or petition of a confined person shall be obliged to consider it within the time periods established by law, to take necessary measures, and to inform the complainant of his decision.

A procurator shall be obliged to see that complaints and petitions of confined persons are dispatched without delay by the administration of places of deprivation of freedom to those agencies or those officials to whom they are addressed.

Article 37. The administration of a place of deprivation of freedom shall be obliged to carry out proposals of a procurator regarding observance of the rules established by law for the keeping of confined persons.*

6. CORRECTIVE LABOR LEGISLATION OF THE U.S.S.R.

The following excerpts are from Soviet materials on corrective labor, from "Fundamentals of Corrective Labor Legislation of the U.S.S.R." (issued in 1969, published in pamphlet form in 1970).

Article 1. The Tasks of Soviet Corrective Labor Legislation. The task of corrective labor legislation is to secure the carrying out of criminal punishment in order not only that it should be a penalty for a crime that has been committed but also that it should correct and reform those who have been convicted, in the spirit of an honest attitude toward labor, exact compliance with the laws, and respect for the rules of socialist communal life, should deter the commission of new crime both by those who have been convicted and by others, and also should foster the eradication of crime.

The carrying out of punishment does not have as a purpose the causing of physical suffering or the degradation of human dignity.

Article 36. Securing Material and Daily Living Conditions for Persons Deprived of Freedom. Persons serving out a term of punishment in places of deprivation of freedom shall be secured the necessary conditions for daily living and housing that correspond to the rules of sanitation and hygiene.

Convicts shall be afforded individual sleeping places and bed appurtenances. They shall be provided with clothing, linen, and foot gear in accordance with the season and with due account of climatic conditions.

Convicts shall receive nourishment that secures normal functional capacity of the organism. Dietary norms shall be differentiated, depending upon climatic conditions at the place where the corrective labor institution is located, the character of the work being carried out by the convicts, and their attitude toward labor. Persons lodged in a disciplinary or punishment cell, in an isolator, in a cell-type building, or in a single cell in a special regime colony shall receive nourishment in accordance with lowered quotas.

Pregnant women, nursing mothers, minors, and persons who are ill shall have improved conditions of housing and daily living set up for them and shall be provided with augmented dietary quotas.

Convicted women who have a conscientious attitude toward

* The preceding five sections are from *Soviet Criminal Law and Procedure: The RSFSR Codes,* 2nd ed., trans. Harold J. Berman and James W. Spindler (Cambridge, Mass., 1972).

work and comply with the regulations of the regime, may, with the approval of the observers' commission, be permitted to live outside the colony during the period they are free from work by reason of their pregnancy and childbirth, and also up until their children reach the age of two years. The system whereby convicted women live outside the colony shall be specified by the corrective labor codes of the Republics.

Convicts who are released from their obligation of work by reason of illness, pregnant women, and nursing mothers, shall be provided with nourishment free during the period they are released from work. Minors, as well as first and second group invalids, shall be provided with food and clothing without pay. Convicts who willfully shirk their work shall have the cost of food and clothing deducted from the sums available on their personal account.

Dietary quotas and arrangements for material and daily living conditions for persons deprived of freedom shall be established by the Council of Ministers of the U.S.S.R.*

* Translated by Leon Lipson.

B. Extracts from Petitions

To: The Procurator General of the U.S.S.R.

FROM: Yulia Dymshitz, on behalf of herself and her father, Mark Yulevich Dymshitz, by her attorney, Telford Taylor

1. The petitioner, Yulia Dymshitz, is a former citizen of the Soviet Union. She emigrated to Israel on August 12, 1973, and is presently a citizen of Israel.

2. Petitioner is the daughter of Mark Dymshitz, a citizen of the Soviet Union presently confined at Perm, No. 36, under a judgment of the Leningrad Municipal Court entered December 24, 1970, sentencing him to death, which was reduced by the Supreme Court of the R.S.F.S.R. to fifteen years deprivation of freedom in a corrective labor colony with a strict regime.

3. Petitioner, deprived of the benefits of the paternal relationship because of her father's confinement under the judgment of December 24, 1970, submits this petition by her attorney, Telford Taylor, for relief as hereinafter set forth.

4. The undersigned, Telford Taylor, is a citizen of the United States and a duly accredited attorney under the laws of the State of New York and the District of Columbia. He is the holder of a power of attorney, sworn to by the petitioner on March 24, 1974, authorizing him to act as her attorney in this matter. A copy of the power of attorney is attached to this petition as Annex A.

5. Permission to submit a petition on behalf of petitioner and others was orally granted to the undersigned by the First Deputy Procurator General on April 5, 1974.

PRAYER FOR RELIEF

6. Petitioner prays that, on the grounds and for the reasons hereinafter set forth, the Procurator General of the U.S.S.R.:

a. exercise his power (U.S.S.R. Statute on the Procuracy, Arts. 23 and 25; R.S.F.S.R. Code of Criminal Procedure, Art. 371) to protest the judgment of the Leningrad City Court under which Mark Dymshitz is confined, and the decision of the Supreme Court of the R.S.F.S.R. on appeal from the aforesaid judgment;

b. exercise his power (U.S.S.R. Statute on the Procuracy, Arts. 32 to 37, inclusive) to inquire into the conditions and circumstances under which Mark Dymshitz is and has been confined, and take such action as is necessary to ensure observance of the rules established by law for the keeping of confined persons; and

c. take such other action, including recommendation of executive clemency, as the interests of justice may require.

STATEMENT

7. The sentence of death was imposed on Mark Dymshitz pursuant to a verdict of the Judicial Board on Criminal Cases of the Leningrad Municipal Court finding Dymshitz guilty under the Criminal Code of the R.S.F.S.R., Article 218–I (possession of firearms and ammunition without appropriate permit; two years); Articles 15, 64(a), and 72 (preparation and/or attempt to commit treason and participation in anti-Soviet organization; death with confiscation of property); Articles 15 and 93–1 (preparation and/or attempt to steal state property on especially large scale; death with confiscation of property); Article 40, aggregation to death with confiscation of property, reduced by the Supreme Court of the R.S.F.S.R. to fifteen years. Dymshitz was arrested on June 15, 1970, and was confined from that date.

8. The above verdict was entered following a trial in which Dymshitz and ten other persons were accused. The trial was held during the period December 15 to 24, 1970. Dymshitz and ten other accused appealed the verdicts against them. Dymshitz is described in the decision of the Supreme Court of the R.S.F.S.R. as "a Jew, expelled from the C.P.S.U. in connection with this case, with higher education."

9. Mark Yulevich Dymshitz was born on May 10, 1927, in Lozovaya of the Kharkovskaya *Oblast*. He is married and the father of two daughters, one of whom is the petitioner. His second daughter also resides in Israel. At the time of his arrest, he was not working but had previously worked in the "Ptitzeprom" trust as a senior engineer. Dymshitz had no previous criminal convictions.

10. The charges against Dymshitz and nine of the other accused, as summarized in the decision of the Supreme Court of the R.S.F.S.R., were that they entered into a criminal agreement in 1969–1970 to escape overseas by hijacking a state-owned airplane and that this plan was motivated by anti-Soviet feelings. This is the basis of the charges under Articles 15, 64(a), and 72, and Articles 15, and 93–1.

11. Dymshitz was also charged with producing and possessing a four-charge revolver without an appropriate permit. This is the basis for the charge under Article 218–1.

PRAYER FOR PROTEST AGAINST THE JUDGMENT

12. The verdict under Articles 15 and 64(a) cannot be sustained. Criminal liability under Article 64(a) requires not only specific action (in this case "flight abroad"), but also that the act be "intentionally committed by a citizen of the U.S.S.R. to the detriment of the state independence, the territorial inviolability, or the military might of the U.S.S.R." The legal issues surrounding the application of Article 64(a) are fully developed in Legal Memorandum IV, which is incorporated herein by reference.

13. The opinion of the Judicial Board on Criminal Matters of the Supreme Court of the R.S.F.S.R. found that the presence of the intention to betray the Motherland had been determined by the aggregation of the materials of the case. But neither the Supreme Court nor the Leningrad City Court cited any evidence indicating that such an intention was directly attributable to Dymshitz. To establish the intent on the part of the accused required by Article 64(a), the Supreme Court of the R.S.F.S.R. relied on four findings: (a) the composition and signing of the so-called "Appeal" which was regarded by the court as anti-Soviet; (b) the preparation and duplication of literature found by the court to be anti-Soviet; (c) the intention to seek political asylum; and (d) the organizational activities directed toward the seizure of the airplane, beginning in Autumn, 1969.

14. The Supreme Court emphasized in particular the signing of the so-called Appeal. But it is undisputed that Dymshitz did not personally sign the Appeal; he was not even present when it was signed. His name was placed on the document by others. The Supreme Court concluded that the charge of treasonable aims was confirmed also by the fact that the majority of the defendants systematically engaged in the preparation and possession of anti-Soviet literature. But Dymshitz was not personally charged with any such conduct. And it is a fundamental doctrine of Soviet law that guilt is personal. No individual defendant can be convicted of a crime on the basis of what a majority of his co-defendants have done.

15. The only evidence of intention mentioned by the Supreme Court which in any way bears on Dymshitz personally is (a) that he participated in the organizational activities leading toward the preparation for the escape for a long period of time; and (b) that he intended to ask the competent authorities in Sweden for political asylum. But both of these actions are entirely consistent with a violation by a Soviet citizen of Article 83 of the Criminal Code of the R.S.F.S.R., and they do not rise to the level of a violation of

Article 64. This argument is supported by Legal Memorandum IV and by paragraphs 16 to 19 below.

16. Article 83 makes it a crime for anyone to "exit abroad . . . without the requisite passport or the permission of the proper authorities . . . ," punishable by three years deprivation of freedom. It is obvious that any Soviet citizen who seeks to exit abroad without passport or permission must necessarily intend to seek political asylum in another country. If evidence of an intention to seek political asylum were to be regarded as sufficient to convert an illegal exit (under Article 83) into an act of treason (under Article 64), then Article 83 would be rendered superfluous with regard to Soviet citizens. Therefore, in order for an illegal exit to be considered treason, it is not enough that the person merely wanted to leave the U.S.S.R. and relocate elsewhere.

17. Indeed, the courts in this case explicitly recognized this in the case of Bodnia, where they concluded that there was no information proving Bodnia's anti-Soviet intention. The court concluded therefore that he was merely guilty of wanting to escape under Article 15, part I. But it is beyond dispute that Bodnia also intended to seek political asylum. How else could he have joined his mother abroad? It is clear, therefore, that evidence of an intent to seek asylum is insufficient to convert an illegal exit under Article 83 into treason under Article 64.

18. Moreover, the mere fact that Dymshitz participated in the planning of the escape is not sufficient to sustain a finding of a treasonous purpose. Participating in planning an escape is consistent with a violation of Article 83. An escape from the Soviet Union by a Soviet citizen—whether in violation of Article 83 or Article 64—requires extensive planning and organization. The mere fact of such planning and organization reveals nothing about the purpose of the escape. Again the Bodnia case is conclusive on this issue. Bodnia also participated in the planning for the escape. He too had a designated role in the complex plan. But he was convicted under Article 83, and not under Article 64.

19. Thus, the evidence of anti-Soviet motive—the essential fact that converts a violation of Article 83 into a violation of Article 64 —is as lacking in Dymshitz's case as it was in Bodnia's case. There is simply no evidence of this issue attributable personally to Dymshitz that would not be equally attributable to Bodnia.* The two

* The Leningrad City Court mentioned that Dymshitz had intended to speak at a news conference when seeking asylum. There was no evidence that Bodnia did not also intend to participate in this event. Moreover, there was no evidence of what Dymshitz would have said. In any event the Supreme Court did not mention this evidence in its findings.

cases are indistinguishable on this issue. It follows, therefore, that Dymshitz's conviction under Article 64 must be vacated; he may be convicted only under Article 83 which carries a maximum penalty of three years.

20. The verdict under Article 93–1 cannot be sustained. Article 93–1 applies to the "stealing" of state or social property. It is a fundamental principle of law that the temporary taking of property without an intent to keep it is not stealing. Stealing requires an intention to deprive the owner of the property of its use permanently, and not for a brief period of time. It is undisputed that the plan in this case called for landing of the plane in Sweden and its abandonment there in a public place. There can be no doubt that the plane would have been returned to the Soviet Union within hours. Thus, if the plan had succeeded, it is clear that no theft would have occurred. It follows, therefore, that since the plan failed, there cannot be a conviction under Articles 15 and 93–1.

21. Moreover, the subsequent enactment of a statute specifically prohibiting the hijacking of airplanes demonstrates that Article 93–1 was not intended to cover such crimes. This argument is developed in Legal Memorandum IV, which is incorporated by reference herein.

22. The punishment was excessive in light of the failure of the plan. It is undisputed that the harm that Dymshitz was allegedly planning did not occur: there was no escape; there was no theft; and there was no harm caused to the Soviet Union.

It is a fundamental principle of Soviet law that the less proximate a criminal act is to the ultimate harm, the lower the punishment should be. Accordingly, the fifteen-year penalty imposed on Dymshitz in this case should be reduced (perhaps by application of Article 43 of the R.S.F.S.R. criminal code) to reflect the undisputed fact that the defendant did not come close to perpetrating the ultimate harm he was allegedly planning. This point is developed in Legal Memorandum IV, which is incorporated here by reference.

23. Dymshitz was denied his rights under Article 51 of the Criminal Procedure Code (Duties and Rights of Defense Counsel). Dymshitz's advocate refused to argue that Article 64 was inapplicable to Dymshitz's conduct. He explicitly told the court that he agreed with the application of that article to Dymshitz's conduct. He confessed Dymshitz's guilt under Article 64, despite Dymshitz's own explicit denial of anti-Soviet intention and despite the complete lack of evidence of anti-Soviet intention on the part of Dymshitz.

24. The Supreme Court explicitly found that Dymshitz denied the guilt of the attempt to betray the Motherland. The City Court also found that Dymshitz did not consider himself guilty of treason

of the Motherland. Yet his advocate refused to argue the inapplicability of the treason article to the court. Instead he told the court that he agreed with its application.

25. Other advocates for other defendants in this case did argue that Article 64 was inapplicable to their clients, on the ground that their clients did not have the requisite anti-Soviet intent. Dymshitz's claim in this regard was far stronger than any of the other defendants with the possible exception of Bodnia, since Dymshitz neither signed the Appeal nor was charged with possession or distribution of anti-Soviet material under Article 70. Yet despite the lack of any evidence of anti-Soviet intent and in the face of Dymshitz's explicit denial of such an intent, his advocate refused to make this argument. This refusal constituted a denial of Dymshitz's right to be represented by a lawyer on this most critical issue. The right of an accused to be represented by counsel is more fully developed in Legal Memorandum I, which is herein incorporated by reference.

26. Violation of the Right to a Defense. Legal Memorandum I sets forth the legal requirements surrounding the right of the accused to a defense, and is incorporated herein by reference. Based upon that legal memorandum and upon the facts recited in the sworn affidavits attached thereto, Dymshitz was deprived of his right to a defense, as hereinafter indicated.

27. Dymshitz, as well as the other accused, was denied the right to put questions to the witness Mikhail Korenblit. According to the affidavits attached to Legal Memorandum I of Pinchos Knokh and Polina Korenblit, the wife of the witness Korenblit, the following occurred: while Korenblit was testifying under direct examination by the prosecutor, he began to describe what he had observed at Dymshitz's house two days prior to the arrest on June 15, 1970. In the middle of a sentence, the witness Korenblit was interrupted by the chairman of the court and immediately removed from the courtroom. While in the process of being removed, Korenblit attempted to complete his statement as to what he had observed at Dymshitz's home on June 13, 1970. Pinchos Knokh indicates in his affidavit that according to his observation the interruption occurred as Korenblit was beginning to discuss Dymshitz's attitude toward leaving the Soviet Union. Polina Korenblit, the wife of the witness, states in her affidavit that after the trial she discussed with her husband what testimony he would have given had he been permitted to complete his testimony. Her husband informed her that he would have sworn that he had discussed with Dymshitz the infiltration of the group by the KGB in order to stimulate the crime.

28. Korenblit's testimony—had it been given—was relevant on a number of important issues. It might have supported the defend-

ants' claim that their reasons for leaving the Soviet Union were not
anti-Soviet. And it would have supported the argument that the Soviet authorities knew about the hijack plan well before June 15,
1970.

29. The denial to Dymshitz of the right to question the witness
Korenblit on issues relevant to his defense constitutes a violation of
Soviet procedural law, in particular Articles 276 and 283 of the
R.S.F.S.R. Code of Criminal Procedure. This point is developed in
Legal Memorandum I.

30. Grounds of Prayer for Protest. Under Article 379 of the
R.S.F.S.R. Code of Criminal Procedure, the grounds for vacating
a judgment that has taken legal effect are those stated in Article 342
as grounds for cassation. All five of the grounds listed in Article
342 are comprised within the circumstances and arguments set forth
hereinbefore.

31. Prayer for Rectification of Confinement Condition. Affidavits have been submitted by other petitioners regarding the conditions of confinement at Perm, and Legal Memorandum III has been
submitted regarding the rules established by law for the keeping of
confined persons. These documents are incorporated herein by
reference. . . .

33. The petitioner's affidavit, like numerous other affidavits submitted in connection with other petitions, declares that Dymshitz,
a Jew, is confined in company with former Nazi convicts. These
former Nazis occupy positions in the camp in which they exercise
authority over Dymshitz. The prison officials at Perm, number 36,
permit these former Nazis to engage in anti-Semitic taunting of
Dymshitz and other Jewish prisoners.

34. The petitioner's affidavit also indicates that prison authorities
have confiscated some of Dymshitz's letters to his family.

35. Petitioner's prayer that the Procurator General exercise his
power under Articles 32 to 37 of the statute on the Procuracy is
based on this affidavit and the legal memorandum on the rules
established by law for the keeping of confined persons, submitted by
the undersigned and designated Legal Memorandum III.

PRAYER FOR EXECUTIVE CLEMENCY OR OTHER RELIEF

36. Petitioner is aware that, under Article 33–1 of the Constitution of the R.S.F.S.R., the power of pardon is vested in the Presidium of the Supreme Soviet of the R.S.F.S.R. for citizens, such
as Dymshitz, who have been convicted by a judicial agency of the
R.S.F.S.R. Petitioner has also taken note of the information in the
officially approved textbook *Ispravitel' notrudovoe pravo* (Moscow,
1971), that the grounds of and procedure for invoking clemency
are not prescribed by statute, and that the initiative for seeking

clemency may derive from relatives of the convicted person, or from any organ of governmental power (pp. 371–373). It is also stated therein that clemency may accord either full or partial relief from unfulfilled portions of the sentence.

37. Accordingly, petitioner prays that, insofar as the other prayers of this petition may not be granted, this petition be regarded also as an initiative for clemency, and transmitted to the appropriate official of the Presidium of the Supreme Soviet of the U.S.S.R.

38. In support of the initiative for clemency, petitioner respectfully emphasizes that, having been permitted to emigrate, she is living in Israel; that she has great need for the parental association of which she has been deprived by Dymshitz's confinement in the Soviet Union; and that he has in fact caused no harm to the Soviet State or its people, and would present no danger to them when reunited with his family.

39. Petitioner also prays that the Procurator General take whatever other action in this matter the interests of justice may require.

Respectfully submitted,

TELFORD TAYLOR
June, 1974   Attorney for Petitioner

ANNEX A

I, Yulia Dymshitz, daughter of Mark Dymshitz, currently interned in a labor camp in the U.S.S.R. by verdict of the City Court, and being deprived of the companionship and guidance of my father, hereby empower Mr. Telford Taylor of New York City, New York State, U.S.A., to act in my behalf as my attorney to petition for the release of my father, amelioration of the conditions of his incarceration, and to consult with any attorney he may deem appropriate and useful to accomplish this goal.

Yulia Dymshitz
March 20, 1974

PETITION

To: The Procurator General of the U.S.S.R.

FROM: Avraham Zalmanson, on behalf of himself and his nephew Eduard Samvilovich Kuznetsov, by his attorney, Telford Taylor

1. The petitioner, Avraham Zalmanson, is a former citizen of the Soviet Union, and is presently a citizen of Israel.

2. Petitioner is the uncle of Eduard Samvilovich Kuznetsov, a citizen of the Soviet Union presently confined at Potma under a judgment of the Leningrad Municipal Court entered December 24,

1970, as modified on appeal, sentencing him to fifteen years deprivation of freedom in a corrective labor colony with a special regime. . . .

STATEMENT

9. Eduard Samvilovich Kuznetsov was born on January 29, 1939, in Moscow. He is married to Silva Zalmanson, and the petitioner is his uncle. At the time of his arrest, he was working as a therapist in the Republican Psychiatric Hospital of Riga. . . .

11. Kuznetsov and five of the others accused were also charged with possession, preparation, duplication, and distribution of anti-Soviet literature. This is the basis for the charge under Article 70–1.

PRAYER FOR PROTEST AGAINST THE JUDGMENT

12. The verdict under Article 70 cannot be sustained. The decision of the R.S.F.S.R. Supreme Court confirming the verdict against Kuznetsov (and the others accused) under Article 70 is based on the determination that the literature prepared, duplicated, and distributed by Kuznetsov and the others was "anti-Soviet" in nature. Also the decision confirming the verdict against Kuznetsov (and the others accused) under Articles 15 and 64(a) is based in part on the conclusion that the accused were guilty under Article 70. Article 70 requires, as an element of the offense, that the propaganda be circulated "for the purpose of subverting or weakening the Soviet regime or of committing particular, especially dangerous crimes against the state," and also describes as criminal the circulation or possession, with that purpose, of "slanderous fabrications which defame the Soviet state and social system."

13. The R.S.F.S.R. Supreme Court's decision, in the case of Kuznetsov, describes as anti-Soviet literature possessed and distributed by him the following: *The Memoirs of Maxim Litvinov,* authorship unspecified; *The Political Leaders of Russia,* by Shub; *The "Appeal,"* by several of the accused; and *Iton.*

14. The documents listed in paragraph 13, together with a few other named documents, were also the documents relied on by the R.S.F.S.R. Supreme Court in affirming the verdict against all the others accused under Article 70, and against the accused under Articles 15 and 64(a).

15. The determination that the literature was anti-Soviet in character within the meaning of Article 70 was invalid, and was made in violation of the articles of the R.S.F.S.R. Code of Criminal Procedure. In support of this statement petitioner respectfully refers to the general memorandum on the legal requirements for establishing the anti-Soviet character of literature, submitted by the undersigned

in support of this and other petitions and designated Legal Memorandum II.

16. Attached to Legal Memorandum II are affidavits sworn to in March of 1973 by Sonia Druk (E–1) and Eva Lisitzin (F–1), petitioners on behalf of their brother Josif Mendelevich, a co-defendant in this proceeding, and by Pinchos Knokh (B–1), petitioner on behalf of his brother Leib Knokh, a co-defendant in this proceeding.

17. The decision of the R.S.F.S.R. Supreme Court recites no basis for the conclusion that the literature relied upon at the trial was anti-Soviet. The affidavits listed in paragraph 16 establish that:

a. no testimony, expert or otherwise,* or any evidence establishing the anti-Soviet character of the literature was received at trial;

b. no references to any prior determination regarding the anti-Soviet character of the literature were contained in any protocols read at the trial;

c. no references to any prior determination regarding the anti-Soviet character of the literature were made by the prosecutor or by the judge at trial; and

d. some of the accused disputed that the literature was anti-Soviet in nature.

18. As is more fully shown in Legal Memorandum II, the circumstances set forth in paragraph 17 establish violations of the R.S.F.S.R. Code of Criminal Procedure. The circumstances also support the conclusion that the charge under Article 70 has not been proven and cannot be the basis of a valid verdict against Kuznetsov; and that the charge under Articles 15 and 64(a), insofar as it was based in part on the possession and distribution of literature declared by the court to be anti-Soviet, has not been proven.

19. The verdict under Articles 15 and 64(a) cannot be sustained. Criminal liability under Article 64(a) requires not only specific action (in this case "flight abroad"), but also that the act be "intentionally committed by a citizen of the U.S.S.R. to the detriment of the state independence, the territorial inviolability, or the military might of the U.S.S.R." The legal issues surrounding the application of Article 64(a) are fully developed in Legal Memorandum IV, which is herein incorporated by reference.

20. To establish the intent on the part of the accused required by Article 64(a), the Supreme Court of the R.S.F.S.R. relied on four

* In contrast, as the affidavits listed in paragraph 16 establish, expert opinion was received on other issues at the trial, including the issue of the categorization of the revolver carried by Dymshits and the issue of the mental health of two of the accused, Mendelevich and Fedorov.

findings: (a) the composition and signing of the so-called "Appeal," which was regarded by the court as anti-Soviet; (b) the preparation and duplication of literature found by the court to be anti-Soviet; (c) the intention to seek political asylum; and (d) the organizational activities directed toward the seizure of the airplane, beginning in autumn 1969.

21. For the reasons set out in paragraphs 12 to 18, and in Legal Memorandum II, it is submitted that the court's conclusion that the "Appeal" and the other documents set out in paragraph 13 were anti-Soviet was improperly arrived at in violation of the R.S.F.S.R. Code of Criminal Procedure and hence cannot be used to support the finding of anti-Soviet purpose. . . .

26. Finally, participating in the planning of the escape is entirely consistent with a violation of Article 83 of the Criminal Code of the R.S.F.S.R. (exit abroad). An escape from the Soviet Union by a Soviet citizen—whether in violation of Article 83 or Article 64— requires extensive planning and organization. The mere fact of such planning and organization reveals nothing about the purpose of the escape. If evidence of planning and organization were to be regarded as sufficient to convert an illegal exit (under Article 83) into an act of treason (under Article 64), then Article 83 would be rendered superfluous with regard to Soviet citizens. Therefore, in order for an illegal exit to be considered treason, it is not enough that the person merely participated in a plan to leave the U.S.S.R. and relocate elsewhere. Again the Bodnia case is conclusive on this issue. Bodnia also participated in the planning for the escape. He too had a designated role in the complex plan. But he was convicted under Article 83, and not under Article 64. . . .

PETITION

To: The Procurator General of the U.S.S.R.

From: Liuba Murzhenko, on behalf of herself and her husband, Alexei Grigoryevich Murzhenko, by her attorney, Telford Taylor

1. The petitioner is a citizen of the Soviet Union.

2. The petitioner is the wife of Alexei Grigoryevich Murzhenko, a citizen of the Soviet Union presently confined under a judgment of the Leningrad Municipal Court entered December 24, 1970, sentencing him to fourteen years deprivation of freedom in a corrective labor colony with a special regime. . . .

9. Alexei Grigoryevich Murzhenko was born on November 3,

1942, in Lozovaya, Kharkovskaya *Oblast*. He is married to the petitioner, and has one child. At the time of his arrest, he had not
worked for two months. In 1962 he had been convicted under Articles 70 and 72 of the Criminal Code of the R.S.F.S.R. and sentenced
to six years deprivation of freedom. . . .

PRAYER FOR PROTEST AGAINST THE JUDGMENT

14. The Supreme Court's finding that Murzhenko's purpose in
seeking to leave the U.S.S.R. was anti-Soviet cannot be supported on
either of the other two bases for the finding. Murzhenko was not
charged personally with intent to seek political asylum and under
Soviet law guilt must be personal. Murzhenko cannot be found to
have anti-Soviet intent because others accused were found to have
an intent to seek political asylum.

15. The only other evidence of intention mentioned by the Supreme Court which in any way bears on Murzhenko personally was
that he participated in the organizational preparation for the escape.
The Supreme Court emphasized that the organizational activities in
preparation for the escape were conducted for a long period of time,
starting from autumn 1969. But Murzhenko did not join in the alleged plan until after April 10, 1970. To the extent that the long-
term character of participation in an organization may be evidence
of intent, the inference cannot apply to Murzhenko. . . .

19. Apart from the four bases for the finding of the requisite intent under Article 64(a) relied upon by the Supreme Court of the
R.S.F.S.R., the Leningrad City Court makes a reference to other
facts in regard to Murzhenko (not repeated in the opinion of the
Supreme Court). The Leningrad City Court refers to Murzhenko's
past conviction and confinement in an attempt to refute Murzhenko's statement that his attempt to escape overseas was not as a
traitor to the Motherland. But, as discussed in paragraphs 20 to 22,
these references are insufficient to support the conclusion that Murzhenko sought to escape in order to harm the Soviet Union.

20. The Leningrad City Court stated that Murzhenko did not become a 100% Soviet man. But this is not in itself a crime under
Soviet law. Nor does it bear directly on what Murzhenko may have
intended to do once he left the country. Not being a 100% Soviet
man may be relevant on the issue of whether Murzhenko intended to
leave the Soviet Union; but that issue is not in dispute. The only
relevant question is whether he intended to engage in activities harmful to the external security of the State once he was abroad. But the
mere fact of being less than a 100% Soviet man does not prove
such intent. Otherwise any former criminal or less than 100% Soviet

man who seeks to leave the country illegally automatically violates
Article 64(a) rather than Article 83, regardless of his intention.

21. The Leningrad City Court also states that Murzhenko's former conviction in 1962 was one of his "motives" for escaping overseas. But there is no explanation of how the fact that Murzhenko
was previously convicted demonstrates that Murzhenko intended to
harm the Soviet Union, and therefore was a traitor. This reference
by the Leningrad City Court appears to be an improper attempt to
place Murzhenko in double jeopardy for acts committed eight years
previously, when he was less than twenty years old.

22. The Leningrad City Court also found confirmation for its
conclusion that Murzhenko was a traitor in the fact that Murzhenko
allegedly led a parasitic way of life while serving a term of punishment for anti-Soviet activities. Significantly, there was not even an
allegation that Murzhenko led a parasitic way of life after he was
released from confinement, in the period preceding his involvement
in the hijacking plan. Moreover, parasitism is a crime separate and
distinct from the grave crime of treason. Mentioning it in this context appears to be a further improper attempt to subject Murzhenko
to double jeopardy.

23. The conclusion that Murzhenko was not acting as a traitor
to the Motherland is further strengthened by the absence of any
proof of his connection with alleged anti-Soviet organizations and
publications in the years immediately prior to his arrest.

24. Accordingly, for the reasons set forth in paragraphs 12 to 23,
there is no evidence cited in the Supreme Court's decision which can
properly support the conclusion that Murzhenko's desire to leave the
U.S.S.R. involved an anti-Soviet purpose. . . .

PETITION

To: The Procurator General of the U.S.S.R.
From: Valery Vudka, on behalf of himself and his brother, Yuri
Vudka, by his attorney, Telford Taylor

1. The petitioner, Valery Vudka, is a former citizen of the Soviet
Union. He emigrated to Israel in February 1973, and is presently a
citizen of Israel resident in Holon, Kiryat-Sharet.

2. Petitioner is the younger brother of Yuri Vudka, a citizen of
the Soviet Union presently confined in prison at Vladimir under a
verdict of the Judicial Board for Criminal Cases of the Ryazan District Court entered on February 19, 1970, sentencing him to seven
years' confinement in a corrective labor colony with a strict regime.

3. Petitioner, deprived of the benefits of the fraternal relation because of his brother's confinement under the judgment of February

19, 1970, submits this petition, by his attorney, Telford Taylor, for relief as hereinafter set forth. . . .

Statement

7. The sentence of seven years' imprisonment was imposed upon Yuri Vudka pursuant to a verdict of the Ryazan District Court finding him guilty under the Criminal Code of the R.S.F.S.R., Articles 70, paragraph 1, and 72 (participation in anti-Soviet agitation, propaganda, and organization).

8. The above verdict was entered following a trial in which Yuri Vudka and five other persons (one of whom was the petitioner) were accused. The trial was held during the period February 9 to 19, 1970. The verdict was affirmed on appeal to the Supreme Court of the R.S.F.S.R.

9. Yuri Veniaminovich Vudka was born on October 30, 1947, in Pavlograd. He is described in the judgment of the R.S.F.S.R. Supreme Court as "a Jew, non-Party, with uncompleted higher education." He studied at the Ryazan Radiotechnical Institute and at the time of his arrest was working as a lathe operator at the "Ryaselmash" factory and residing in Ryazan. Vudka had no previous criminal convictions.

10. The charges against Yuri Vudka and the other defendants were that they formed an "organization" which engaged in the illegal activity of preparing and distributing anti-Soviet literature, in violation of Articles 70, paragraphs 1 and 72.

Prayer for Protest Against the Judgment

11. *Violation of Articles 240 and 301 of the R.S.F.S.R. Code of Criminal Procedure.* The verdict against Vudka under Articles 70, paragraph 1, and 72 is based on the determination that the literature circulated by him and the others accused was "anti-Soviet" in character. Article 70 requires, as an element of the offense, that the propaganda be circulated "for the purpose of subverting or weakening the Soviet regime or of committing particular, dangerous crimes against the State," and also describes as criminal the circulation or possession, with that purpose, of slanderous fabrications which defame the Soviet State and social system.

12. The determination that the literature was anti-Soviet in character within the meaning of Article 70 was invalid, and was made in violation of the articles of the R.S.F.S.R. Code of Criminal Procedure listed in paragraph 11. In support of this statement, petitioner respectfully refers to the general memorandum on the legal requirements for establishing the anti-Soviet character of literature, submitted by the undersigned in support of this and other petitions and designated Legal Memorandum II.

13. Attached to Legal Memorandum II are affidavits sworn to in March 1973 by the petitioner (R–1) and by Aaron Grilius (P–1) (father of Shimon Grilius, a co-defendant in this proceeding). These affidavits declare that:

    a. no testimony, expert or otherwise, was presented at the trial to support a determination that the literature in question was anti-Soviet;

    b. no reference was made during the trial to any official protocols, memoranda, or other documents characterizing the literature as anti-Soviet;

    c. the trial judge refused to hear testimony by the defendants relating to the content of the materials, and specifically refused to allow Yuri Vudka to read some of it into the record of the trial in order to demonstrate that it was not anti-Soviet.

14. As is more fully set forth in Legal Memorandum II, the circumstances set forth in paragraph 13 establish violations of R.S.F.S.R. Code of Criminal Procedure Articles 240 (obligation of trial courts to analyze evidence, hear opinions of experts, and publicly disclose records and other documents) and 301 (necessary foundations of a valid judgment). . . .

PRAYER FOR RECTIFICATION OF CONFINEMENT CONDITIONS

17. These and other affidavits submitted in connection with other petitions declare that the physical and social circumstances of Vudka's confinement are oppressive and injurious to health, and degrading and injurious to human dignity, in that Vudka and other Jewish convicts are confined in company with Nazi collaborators who subject them to humiliation and abuse. It is also set forth therein that Vudka has suffered oppressive measures because of his observation of Jewish religious rules with respect to food and attire, in apparent violation of Article 143 of the R.S.F.S.R. Criminal Code.

18. Petitioner's prayer that the Procurator General exercise his power under Articles 32 to 37 of the Statute on the Procuracy is based on these affidavits and the legal memorandum on the rules established by law for the keeping of confined persons, submitted by the undersigned and designated Legal Memorandum III.

PETITION

To: The Procurator General of the U.S.S.R.

FROM: Eva Butman, on behalf of herself and her husband, Hillel Butman, by her attorney, Telford Taylor

1. The petitioner, Eva Butman, is a former citizen of the Soviet Union. She emigrated to Israel on July 12, 1973, and is presently a citizen of Israel resident in Jerusalem.

2. Petitioner is the wife of Hillel Butman, a citizen of the Soviet Union presently confined at Camp 35, Perm, under a judgment of the Leningrad Municipal Court entered May 20, 1971, sentencing him to ten years deprivation of freedom in a corrective labor colony with a strict regime.

3. Petitioner, deprived of the benefits of the connubial relationship because of her husband's confinement under the judgment of May 20, 1971, submits this petition, by her attorney, Telford Taylor, for relief as hereinafter set forth.

4. The undersigned, Telford Taylor, is a citizen of the United States and a duly accredited attorney under the laws of the State of New York and the District of Columbia. He is the holder of a power of attorney, sworn to by the petitioner on March 21, 1974, authorizing him to act as her attorney in this matter.

5. Permission to submit a petition in behalf of petitioner and others was orally granted to the undersigned by the First Deputy Procurator General on April 5, 1974.

PRAYER FOR RELIEF

6. Petitioner prays that, on the grounds and for the reasons hereinafter set forth, the Procurator General of the U.S.S.R.:

a. exercise his power (U.S.S.R. Statute on the Procuracy, Articles 23 and 25; R.S.F.S.R. Code of Criminal Procedure, Article 371) to protest the judgment of the Leningrad Municipal Court under which Hillel Butman is confined, and the decision of the Supreme Court of the R.S.F.S.R. denying Butman's appeal from the aforesaid judgment;

b. exercise his power (U.S.S.R. Statute on the Procuracy, Articles 32 to 37 inclusive) to inquire into the conditions and circumstances under which Hillel Butman is and has been confined, and take such action as is necessary to ensure observance of the rules established by law for the keeping of confined persons, and

c. take such other action, including recommendation of executive clemency, as the interests of justice may require.

STATEMENT

7. The sentence of ten years confinement was imposed on Hillel Butman pursuant to a verdict of the Judicial Board on Criminal Cases of the Leningrad Municipal Court finding Butman guilty under the Criminal Code of the R.S.F.S.R., Article 189, paragraph 1 (concealing stolen government property; two years), Articles 70,

paragraph 1, and 72 (participation in anti-Soviet agitation, propaganda, and organization; five years); and complicity in treason (Articles 17 and 64a; aggregation to ten years confinement).

8. Butman was arrested on June 15, 1970, and was confined from that date. The above verdict was entered following a trial in which Butman and eight other persons were accused. The trial was held during the period May 11 to 20, 1971. Butman and seven of the others accused appealed the verdicts against them. Each of the eight is described in the decision of the Supreme Court of the R.S.F.S.R. as "a Jew, non-Party, with higher education."

9. Hillel Israelevich Butman was born on September 11, 1932, in Leningrad. He is married to petitioner, and they have one daughter. He is a graduate of the Leningrad Law Institute and the Leningrad Polytechnic Institute and at the time of his arrest was working as an engineer at the "Eletrik" plant and residing in Leningrad. Butman had no previous criminal convictions.

10. The charges against the nine accused, as summarized in the decision of the Supreme Court of the R.S.F.S.R., were that they formed, beginning late in 1966, an "illegal anti-Soviet and Zionist organization" which "actively conducted propaganda, aimed at undermining and weakening the Soviet regime," primarily by the duplication and distribution of "anti-Soviet literature." This is the basis of the charges under Articles 70 and 72.

11. Butman and six others accused were also charged with utilizing in this work an "ERA" duplicating machine, with knowledge that it had been stolen from a government office in Kishinev. This is the basis for the charge under Article 189.

12. Butman and one other defendant (Mikhail Korenblit) were also accused of complicity in the attempted seizure of a Soviet passenger airplane in order to escape abroad. This accusation is the basis of the charge under Articles 17 and 64(a).

PRAYER FOR PROTEST AGAINST THE JUDGMENT

13. *Violation of Article 50 of the R.S.F.S.R. Code of Criminal Procedure.* . . . As is set forth in petitioner's affidavit, the accused Butman rejected representation by counsel and informed the prosecuting authorities that he wished to conduct his own defense. The accused was himself a graduate of a law institute, and also had experience as a police investigator. Despite the accused's objections, a lawyer chosen by the Leningrad Collegium was appointed to represent him, and the accused was informed that he had no right to refuse the appointed lawyer's services. Thereafter the accused was represented by the appointed lawyer throughout the trial and appeal.

14. The facts set forth in paragraph 13 constitute a clear violation

of Article 50 of the R.S.F.S.R. Code of Criminal Procedure, which provides that: "The accused shall have the right at any moment in the conduct of a case to refuse defense counsel." It is plain from the second paragraph of Article 50 that, unless the defendant is a minor or physically or mentally defective, the accused's refusal of counsel is binding on the court, the investigator, and the procurator. Petitioner also calls attention to the legal memorandum on an accused's right to counsel of his own choice, submitted separately by the undersigned in support of this and other petitions, and designated Legal Memorandum I.

15. *Violation of Articles 184, 185, 240, 276, 289, 292, and 301 of the R.S.F.S.R. Cole of Criminal Procedure.* The decision of the R.S.F.S.R. Supreme Court confirming the verdict against Butman (and the others accused) under Articles 70 and 72 is based in principal part on the determination that the literature duplicated and circulated by Butman and the others was "anti-Soviet" in nature. Article 70 requires, as an element of the offense, that the propaganda be circulated "for the purpose of subverting or weakening the Soviet regime or of committing particular, especially dangerous crimes against the state," and also describes as criminal the circulation or possession with that purpose, of "slanderous fabrications which defame the Soviet state and social system."

16. The R.S.F.S.R. Supreme Court's decision, in the case of Butman, describes as anti-Soviet literature possessed and distributed by him the following: *Exodus,* by Leon Uris; *An Open Letter,* by A. Kenan; *The Aggressors,* by Mnlachko; *Our Tasks,* by the co-defendant Shtilbans; *The Memoirs of Maxim Litvinov,* authorship unspecified in the decision; and *Iton-1* and *Iton-2,* described as "illegal collections of works," authorship and contents unspecified in the decision.

17. The documents listed in paragraph 16, together with a few other named documents, were also the documents relied on by the R.S.F.S.R. Supreme Court in affirming the verdict against all the others accused under Articles 70 and 72.

18. The determination that the literature was anti-Soviet in character within the meaning of Article 70 was invalid, and was made in violation of the articles of the R.S.F.S.R. Code of Criminal Procedure listed in paragraph 15. In support of this statement, petitioner respectfully refers to the general memorandum on the legal requirements for establishing the anti-Soviet character of literature, submitted by the undersigned in support of this and other petitions and designated Legal Memorandum II.

19. Attached to Legal Memorandum II are affidavits sworn to in March of 1973 by Musia Yagman (wife of Lev Yagman, a co-defendant in this proceeding), Polina Korenblit (wife of Mikhail

Korenblit, a co-defendant in this proceeding), Sima Kaminsky (wife of Lassal Kaminsky, a co-defendant in this proceeding), Victor Boguslavsky, and Lev Korenblit (both co-defendants in this proceeding).

20. The decision of the R.S.F.S.R. Supreme Court recites no basis for the conclusion that the literature relied upon at the trial was anti-Soviet. The affidavits listed in paragraph 19 establish that:

a. there was an *Oblit* (or perhaps *Glavlit*) memorandum in Lev Korenblit's dossier (and presumably in the dossiers of the others accused, since the literature was in all cases somewhat the same) describing the literature so relied upon as anti-Soviet;

b. the *Oblit* document was not read publicly into the record of the trial;

c. Lev Korenblit's wish to call witnesses to give testimony on this crucial issue was not followed by his counsel, who regarded the issue as "foreclosed";

d. no testimony or other evidence establishing the anti-Soviet character of the literature was received at the trial;

e. despite the lack of supporting evidence the trial judge publicly declared that the literature was anti-Soviet; and

f. Boguslavsky's request that his investigator produce expert testimony on the issue was refused.

21. As is more fully shown in Legal Memorandum II, the circumstances set forth in paragraph 20 establish violations of R.S.F.S.R. Code of Criminal Procedure Articles 184 and 185 (use of experts during pre-trial investigation); 276 and 289 (calling of expert witnesses at trial); 240 and 292 (public disclosure of documents in the dossier); and 301 (necessary foundations of a valid judgment). The circumstances also support the conclusion that the charge under Articles 70 and 72 has not been proven and cannot be the basis of a valid verdict against Butman.

22. *The charge under Article 189.* As related in the decision of the R.S.F.S.R. Supreme Court, Butman was charged under paragraph 1 of Article 189, for concealing the allegedly stolen ERA duplicating machine. It would appear, however, that this conduct would only support a charge under paragraph 2 of Article 189, which embraces paragraph 1 of Article 90, applicable to the crime concealed, inasmuch as force was not used. The sentence imposed (two years) is the maximum permissible under paragraph 2 of Article 189. In any event, Butman has by now served nearly double the term prescribed by the court under this charge, which therefore cannot furnish the basis for his continued confinement.

23. The verdict under Articles 17 and 64a cannot be sustained. This verdict involves the most serious charge against Butman and

accounts for the ten-year duration of the sentence imposed upon him. The thwarted seizure of a Soviet aircraft for escape to Sweden, which occurred on June 15, 1970, was the principal subject of the earlier trial in Leningrad (December 1970) involving the petitioner Dymshitz and others.

24. In the petitions submitted by the undersigned in behalf of the relatives of nine of the defendants in the first Leningrad trial, it is argued that the violations of procedural requirements and the insufficiency of evidence in that trial require setting aside the verdicts under Articles 15 and 64(a) against those defendants. It is plain that, if those arguments are accepted with respect to those convicted in the first Leningrad trial, *a fortiori* they are applicable to Butman. Those arguments are accordingly incorporated herein by reference.

25. Butman did not participate in the effort of June 15, 1970; it is not disputed that from May 27 until his arrest Butman was away from Leningrad, vacationing with his daughter, although this circumstance is not mentioned in the decision of the R.S.F.S.R. Supreme Court. Consequently, he was not charged with attempt under Article 15, but only with complicity under Article 17.

26. It appears to be established that Butman did in fact participate in planning the escape and the seizure of a Soviet TU-124 aircraft, which was to have taken place early in May, but that this project was abandoned by all those involved in April. The issue of Butman's complicity, therefore, depends upon the evidence of his involvement in the later plan for the use of the smaller AN-2 aircraft, which culminated in the episode of June 15, 1970.

27. The course of events leading up to the episode of June 15, 1970, is described in detail in the decisions in the first Leningrad trial by the Leningrad Municipal Court and the R.S.F.S.R. Supreme Court. It is made clear therein that the plan to seize the AN-2 aircraft was not conceived until approximately June 1, 1970. This was several days after Butman had left Leningrad to go on vacation. Neither of those decisions makes any mention of Butman in connection with the preparation of the effort of June 15, 1970. The decision of the Supreme Court of the R.S.F.S.R. in Butman's case contains nothing establishing Butman's complicity in that affair. The fact that Butman, who earlier that year had been involved in the escape plan, did not join in the June 15 effort, and indeed was not in contact with the group after May 25, is strongly corroborative of his lack of connection. In summary, there is a complete failure of proof of Butman's complicity in the June 15 episode.

28. Criminal liability under Article 64(a) requires not only specific action (in this case "flight abroad"), but also that the act be "intentionally committed by a citizen of the U.S.S.R. to the detriment of the state independence, the territorial inviolability, or

the military might of the U.S.S.R." To establish such intent on the part of the accused in the first Leningrad trial, the Supreme Court of the R.S.F.S.R. relied "in particular" on the signing of "the so-called 'Appeal' of anti-Soviet slanderous content," the intention of four of those defendants to ask for political asylum in Sweden, and the earlier circulation of anti-Soviet literature.

Two of these circumstances are completely lacking in the case of Butman. As the decision of the Leningrad Municipal Court in the first Leningrad case states, the "Appeal" was signed on June 9, 1970, at a time when Butman was on vacation and had been out of touch with the others for two weeks. Butman was likewise absent when certain of the others are alleged to have spoken of seeking political asylum. And proof of the anti-Soviet character of the literature previously circulated was, as shown herein (paragraphs 15 to 21) and in the petitions submitted by the undersigned in connection with the first Leningrad trial, insufficient and vitiated by the several violations of the R.S.F.S.R. Code of Criminal Procedure.

29. Under the circumstances set forth in paragraph 28, even if Butman is assumed to be liable for complicity in the June 15 effort, the requirements of Article 64(a) are not fulfilled. At most there would be complicity under Article 83, punishing unlawful departure from the Soviet Union, which carries a maximum penalty of three years deprivation of freedom.

30. Furthermore, and again assuming that Butman's complicity is established, the complicity related not to a completed offense under Article 64(a), but only to preparation for an attempt. This is shown by the fact that the participants in the hijacking were charged under Article 15 in conjunction with Article 64(a). Accordingly, there was error in charging Butman with Article 17 in direct conjunction with Article 64(a), for this charge must involve a completed offense. The charge being one of complicity in an attempt should be brought under Articles 15, 17, and 64(a). This conclusion is supported by F. G. Burchak, *Ucheniie o souchastii po sovetskomu ugolovnomv pravu* (Kiev, 1969) pp. 182–83 and 192–93. Burchak cites (p. 183) Professor Durmanov's textbook (1962) and Professor Kovalev's commentary (1961) in support of his conclusion.

31. The error described in paragraph 30 is not merely a technical question of pleading. The social danger of complicity in an attempt is less than that of complicity in a completed offense, as Burchak (p. 183) points out. The matter should therefore have been considered as the basis for imposing a lesser sentence on Butman, perhaps by application of Article 43 of the Criminal Code.

32. *Grounds for Prayer for Protest.* Under Article 379 of the R.S.F.S.R. Code of Criminal Procedure, the grounds for vacating a

judgment which has taken legal effect are those stated in Article 342 as grounds for cassation. All five of the grounds listed in Article 342 are comprised within the circumstances and arguments set forth hereinbefore. Furthermore protest appears to be mandated by Article 343–1, in situations where, as here, "expert examination has not been conducted when the conduct of it is legally obligatory. . . ."

PRAYER FOR RECTIFICATION OF CONFINEMENT CONDITIONS

34. This affidavit, like numerous other affidavits submitted in connection with other petitions, declares that Butman, a Jew, is confined in company with Nazi collaborators.

35. The affidavit also describes as inadequate and oppressive the physical and social circumstances of Butman's confinement.

36. Petitioner's prayer that the Procurator General exercise his power under Articles 32 to 37 of the Statute on the Procuracy is based on this affidavit and the legal memorandum on the rules established by law for the keeping of confined persons, submitted by the undersigned and designated Legal Memorandum III.

PRAYER FOR EXECUTIVE CLEMENCY OR OTHER RELIEF

37. Petitioner is aware that, under Article 33–1 of the Constitution of the R.S.F.S.R., the power of pardon is vested in the Presidium of the Supreme Soviet of the R.S.F.S.R. for citizens, such as Butman, who have been convicted by a judicial agency of the R.S.F.S.R. Petitioner has also taken note of the information in the officially approved textbook *Ispravitel' notrudovoe pravo* (Moscow, 1971), pp. 371–373, that the grounds of and procedure for invoking clemency are not prescribed by statute, and that the initiative for seeking clemency may derive from relatives of the convicted person, or from any organ of governmental power. It is also stated therein that clemency may accord either full or partial relief from unfulfilled portions of the sentence.

38. Accordingly, petitioner prays that, insofar as the other prayers of this petition may not be granted, this petition be regarded also as an initiative for clemency, and transmitted to the appropriate officials of the Presidium of the Supreme Soviet of the U.S.S.R.

39. In support of the initiative for clemency, petitioner respectfully emphasizes that, having been permitted to emigrate, she is living in Israel; that she and the child of their marriage have great need for the connubial and parental association of which they are deprived by Butman's confinement in the Soviet Union; and that he has in fact caused no harm to the Soviet State or its people, and would present no danger to them when reunited with his family.

40. Petitioner also prays that the Procurator General take whatever other action in this matter the interests of justice may require.

Respectfully submitted,

TELFORD TAYLOR

June 1974   Attorney for Petitioner

PETITION

TO: The Procurator General of the U.S.S.R.

FROM: Yalta Pinkhasov, on behalf of herself and her husband, Pinkhas Pinkhasov, by her attorney, Telford Taylor

1. The petitioner, Yalta Pinkhasov, is a former citizen of the Soviet Union. She emigrated to Israel on September 26, 1973, and is presently a citizen of Israel, resident in Hadera.

2. Petitioner is the wife of Pinkhas Pinkhasov, a citizen of the Soviet Union, presently confined at Bolshoi Darim, Mab Derbentovsky Rayon No. 5, Kalmikskaya A.S.S.R., under a judgment of the Derbent City Court, entered on November 13, 1973, sentencing him to five years deprivation of freedom. . . .

STATEMENT

7. The sentence of five years deprivation of freedom was imposed on Pinkhas Pinkhasov pursuant to a verdict of the Derbent City Court, finding Pinkhasov guilty under the Criminal Code of the R.S.F.S.R. Article 92 (misappropriation of state property committed through appropriation, embezzlement, or the misuse of one's official position, four years) and Article 156 (deception of purchasers through false reckoning or the marking up of established retail prices, two years).

8. The above verdict was entered following an open trial in which Pinkhasov alone was accused. The petitioner, his wife, did not attend the trial because at the time it took place she and her children had already emigrated to Israel. To the petitioner's knowledge, neither the verdict of the Derbent City Court nor the decision of the cassational appeal to the Supreme Court of the Dagestanskaya A.S.S.R. has been published. Petitioner has not been shown copies of either document. The results of the trial, however, were reported in the Soviet press. Furthermore, petitioner has learned of what transpired at her husband's trial through the testimony of several eyewitnesses who attended it. Affidavits of those eyewitnesses, including that of Riya Mishayeva, one of the two People's Assessors at the trial, are attached hereto.

9. Pinkhasov was arrested on September 9, 1973, and was confined from that date. The trial was held on November 12 and 13,

1973. Pinkhasov appealed the verdict against him to the Supreme Court of the Dagestanskaya A.S.S.R., unaided by his court-selected advocate Ilyaev, who, subjected to intimidation and threats by the authorities, refused to submit the cassational appeal on Pinkhasov's behalf. For that reason, Pinkhasov submitted the appeal himself. On December 11, 1973, Pinkhasov's appeal was considered by the Supreme Court of the Dagestanskaya A.S.S.R. and the verdict of the Derbent City Court was confirmed. No witnesses were invited to appear and both the accused and his advocate were absent on the day the appeal was considered.

10. Pinkhas Pinkhasov was born in 1935, and prior to his confinement resided in Derbent, Dagestan A.S.S.R. He is a Jew, married to petitioner, and they have six children. After eight years of schooling he began work as a carpenter. In 1959 he lost a leg in an accident at work. At the time of his arrest Pinkhasov had had no previous criminal convictions.

11. Early in 1973 Pinkhasov and his family submitted an application with the proper authorities for emigration to Israel. In the summer of that year they received their emigration permits at the OVIR offices in Makhachkala, the capital of Dagestan. Pinkhasov then resigned from work and finalized all his personal business in anticipation of leaving for Israel by the end of September 1973.

12. Between the time Pinkhasov and his family received their exit visas and the time of his arrest on September 9, 1973, Pinkhasov was repeatedly subjected to demands by the local Derbent authorities, including Investigator Nagiev, that he and his family give up their emigration plans. Pinkhasov was warned that the Arabs would conquer Israel, that it would be dangerous for his children to live there, and that people in Israel are forced to sleep out in the open because of a lack of housing. When, on September 9, 1973, Pinkhasov made clear to the authorities that he would not change his plan to emigrate to Israel, he was arrested in the presence of his wife and children at the local militia station. Not until three days later was the petitioner informed by the authorities of the charges against her husband.

PRAYER FOR PROTEST AGAINST THE JUDGMENT

13. The verdict under Articles 92 and 156 cannot be sustained. From the affidavits of three eyewitnesses to the trial it is clear that no evidence was presented by the prosecution at Pinkhasov's trial that in any way tended to incriminate the accused. On the contrary, all of the prosecution's witnesses insisted that Pinkhasov was innocent. In his affidavit, Yaakov Nissan, brother-in-law of the accused, states that approximately eleven persons for whom Pinkhasov had done carpentry work were called as witnesses by the prosecution

to testify against Pinkhasov. Not one witness, however, substantiated the accusation that Pinkhasov had overcharged his customers.
All testified that Pinkhasov had charged only the correct official
price determined by his factory. They further testified that any additional payments or gifts of food or drink made to Pinkhasov were
due him for additional work which he had performed for them, such
as for the transportation of materials, for overtime and Sunday
work, and for the use of his son as an assistant. No witness complained about these additional payments; all thought them fully
justified. For the defense, there were no witnesses called except
Pinkhasov himself, who denied his guilt completely. When he attempted to state his belief that he was being persecuted in retaliation for his plan to emigrate to Israel, the judge interrupted and
forbade him to speak.

14. Even more convincing in its indication of Pinkhasov's innocence is the affidavit of Riya Mishayeva, who served as a People's
Assessor at the trial of Pinkhasov in November, 1973, and is now
a resident of Israel. In her affidavit Mishayeva states that after
listening carefully to the testimony of the witnesses who were called
by the prosecution, she became convinced of Pinkhasov's innocence.
Furthermore, based upon statements made to her by Judge Rasmasanov and by the other People's Assessor, Mishayeva came to
realize that Pinkhasov was being prosecuted because he had made
application to emigrate to Israel. At one point, during a recess in
the trial, Mishayeva was even asked to carry a message to the accused's family from the judge that if Pinkhasov would give up his
emigration plans and retrieve his wife and children from Israel, the
prosecution against him would be dropped and he would be given
a new apartment and a new job. The affidavit of Yaakov Nissan
corroborates this last point.

15. At his trial, as indicated by Mishayeva's affidavit, Pinkhasov
requested permission to call witnesses on his behalf, but, though
eleven witnesses testified for the prosecution, the judge would not
permit even one witness to appear for the defense. By thereby depriving Pinkhasov of his right to present any evidence at trial, Judge
Rasmasanov clearly violated Articles 46, 51, 245, and 276 of the
R.S.F.S.R. Code of Criminal Procedure. Even more importantly, as
the affidavit of Mishayeva once more makes clear, the testimony
presented by the prosecution witnesses completely failed to substantiate either of the charges leveled against Pinkhasov, yet at the
conclusion of the trial Judge Rasmasanov and the other People's
Assessor nevertheless prepared a guilty verdict which did not correspond to the testimony of the witnesses. In so doing, they violated
Article 301 of the R.S.F.S.R. Code of Criminal Procedure, which

requires a judgment to be reasoned, well-founded, and based only on evidence which has been considered at the trial.

16. *Denial of Pinkhasov's right to counsel of his choice and to a defense.* As indicated by the affidavit of Yaakov Nissan, Pinkhasov's family desired him to be represented at his trial by an advocate from Moscow named Wexler. The local Derbent authorities, however, refused to allow Wexler to represent Pinkhasov and insisted that only a local advocate, Ovadya Ilyaev, could serve as Pinkhasov's lawyer. Intimidated and threatened by the authorities, Ilyaev presented only a token defense on behalf of the accused and flatly refused to submit a cassational appeal. Since the other lawyer in Derbent was unwilling to represent Pinkhasov, the accused had to prepare his own cassational complaint. Pinkhasov's cassational appeal was considered by the Supreme Court of the Dagestanskaya A.S.S.R. on December 11, 1973. The witnesses were not invited to the hearing, nor did Advocate Ilyaev appear. Pinkhasov himself was not allowed to attend. After fifteen minutes of consideration, the court confirmed the verdict of the Derbent City Court. Though a further appeal to the Supreme Court of the R.S.F.S.R. was theoretically possible, Pinkhasov and his family could find no one to represent him in an appeal to that court. . . .

PETITION

To: The Procurator General of the U.S.S.R.

From: Feiga Moiseevna Shkolnik, on behalf of herself and her husband, Isaac Rafailovich Shkolnik, by her attorney, Telford Taylor

1. The petitioner, Feiga Shkolnik, is a former citizen of the Soviet Union. She emigrated to Israel on December 31, 1973, and is presently a citizen of Israel, resident in Beersheva.

2. Petitioner is the wife of Isaac Shkolnik, a citizen of the Soviet Union presently confined at Camp 35, Perm, under a judgment of the Military Tribunal of the Cis-Carpathian Military District, Vinnitsa, entered on April 11, 1973, sentencing him to ten years, reduced on appeal of sentence to seven years, deprivation of freedom.

3. The petitioner, deprived of the benefits of the connubial relationship because of her husband's confinement under the judgment of April 11, 1973, submits this petition, by her attorney, Telford Taylor, for relief as hereinafter set forth. A copy of the power of attorney is attached to this petition as Annex A.

4. Permission to submit a petition in behalf of petitioner and others was orally granted to the undersigned by the First Deputy Procurator General on April 5, 1974. . . .

5. Petitioner prays that . . . the Procurator General shall . . . :

c. exercise his power under the Statute on Procuracy Supervision in the U.S.S.R., Arts. 32 to 37, inclusive, to produce for the inspection of the undersigned the verdicts and decisions in this case, and

d. take such other action, including recommendation of executive clemency, as the interests of justice may require.

STATEMENT

6. The sentence of ten years confinement was imposed on Isaac Shkolnik pursuant to a verdict of the Military Tribunal of the Cis-Carpathian Military District, Vinnitsa, Ukraine S.S.R., finding Shkolnik guilty under the Criminal Code of the Ukraine, Article 56 (equivalent to Article 64 of the Criminal Code of the R.S.F.S.R.: treason, ten years) and Article 62 (equivalent to Article 70 of the Criminal Code of the R.S.F.S.R.: anti-Soviet agitation and propaganda, five years), aggregation to ten years, reduced to seven years confinement.

7. The above verdict was entered following an in camera (closed) trial in which Shkolnik alone was accused. Shkolnik's trial, being before a military tribunal, was not open to the relatives of the accused. The petitioner, his wife, was not permitted to attend except for the period during which she herself appeared as a witness for her husband. To the petitioner's knowledge, neither the verdict of the military tribunal nor the decision of the cassational appeal has been made public. Petitioner has not been shown copies of either document. The results of the trial were, however, reported in the Soviet press. This petition is based largely upon information reported in the Soviet press, upon the affidavits of the petitioner attached hereto, and upon previous applications of the petitioner, also attached hereto.

8. Shkolnik was arrested on July 5, 1972, and was confined from that date. The trial was held during the period March 29 to April 11, 1973. Shkolnik appealed the verdict against him, and on June 13, 1973, the petitioner wrote to the Presidium of the Supreme Soviet of the U.S.S.R. and to the Secretary General of the Central Committee of the C.P.S.U. (with a copy to the Military Board of the Supreme Court of the U.S.S.R.) requesting reconsideration and repeal of Shkolnik's sentence. A copy of the June 13, 1973, request is attached hereto as Annex B.

9. Isaac Rafailovich Shkolnik was born in 1936, and prior to his confinement resided in Vinnitsa, Ukraine. He is a Jew, married to petitioner, and they have one young daughter. Shkolnik had no secondary or specialized education. He had worked as a laborer,

as a miner, and as a mechanic. At the time of his arrest, he was working as a fitter at an automatic appliances factory in Vinnitsa. Shkolnik had no previous criminal convictions.

10. At the time of his arrest on July 5, 1972, Shkolnik's apartment was searched. The materials seized included letters written in the English language, received by Shkolnik from Canada and England, cards and photographs with English writing, various magazines in Russian and English, five American dollars, a customs slip for an imported transistor, a radio, and some handwritten Hebrew lessons. Among the seized items was a visiting card of a British engineer who had been in Vinnitsa in approximately 1968 as part of a group of British engineers who had worked in the Sverdlov Chemical Works of Vinnitsa in order to install equipment which had been purchased from England.

11. After his arrest, Shkolnik was initially charged with a violation of Article 187 of the Criminal Code of the Ukrainian S.S.R. (equivalent to Article 190 of the Criminal Code of the R.S.F.S.R.; systematic circulation in oral form of fabrications known to be false which defame the Soviet state and social system). Subsequently this charge was changed to a charge that Shkolnik had violated Article 62 of the Ukrainian Criminal Code (equivalent to Article 70 of the R.S.F.S.R. Criminal Code: anti-Soviet agitation and propaganda). After approximately six to seven months of pretrial confinement, a new charge was brought against Shkolnik. He was charged under Article 56 of the Criminal Code of the Ukrainian S.S.R. (equivalent to Article 64 of the R.S.F.S.R. Criminal Code) with spying for the British government. When the petitioner, Shkolnik's wife, was informed by the KGB investigator of the new charge, she sent a petition to the Procurator General of the U.S.S.R., requesting that he investigate the belated change in the charges against her husband. In that petition, attached hereto as Annex C, the petitioner declared that she, having known her husband well and for a long period of time, knew that her husband had not engaged in, and had not had the opportunity to engage in, espionage for the British government.

12. In February 1973 the British government learned that Shkolnik had been charged by Soviet authorities with spying for Britain. Representatives of the British government denied that Shkolnik had been an espionage agent for Britain. A member of the British Parliament, Greville Janner, Labour M.P. for Leicester North-West, made this information public, and it was reported in the British press, articles appearing in *The Times* of London (2/12; 2/13; 4/13), the Daily *Telegraph* (2/12; 3/30), the *Daily Mail* (2/12; 4/9; 4/12), and the *Guardian* (2/13). According to these articles,

the British foreign office communicated with Soviet authorities regarding the Shkolnik case, denying that Shkolnik had any connection with Britain.

13. When Shkolnik was brought to trial, commencing March 29, 1973, the charge against him was revised. He was not charged with spying for the British government; rather he was accused of spying for the Israeli government, in violation of Article 56 of the Ukrainian Criminal Code. He was also charged with anti-Soviet agitation and propaganda, in violation of Article 62 of the Ukrainian Criminal Code.

14. As reported in the *Soviet Weekly* on April 21, 1973, the principal charge against Shkolnik at the trial was that he "persistently collected espionage material about the Soviet Union with a view to selling it to Israeli intelligence when he arrived in Israel." The local Ukrainian-language newspaper in Vinnitsa described the principal charge similarly, reporting that Shkolnik was charged with "systematically collecting information for several years regarding the armed forces of the U.S.S.R. in order to transfer the information to one of the foreign secret services." This charge was the basis for the charge under Article 56, Ukraine Criminal Code (Article 64, R.S.F.S.R. Criminal Code).

15. The particular information that Shkolnik was charged with collecting was reported by the *Soviet Weekly* of April 21, 1973, to cover matters "constituting military and state secrets, including: the location and purpose of important defense installations, the location and armament of military units, information on enterprises manufacturing defense equipment, specifications of samples of military equipment of the Soviet Army, including tanks and aircraft."

16. The verdict of treason appears unjustifiable. Without having access to the court documents in this case, the undersigned cannot determine with any assurance what evidence was relied upon to support the conclusion that Shkolnik was guilty of treason. However, the information available to the undersigned from reports in the Soviet press and from the statements of the petitioner suggest certain legal defects in the judgment, as hereinafter indicated.

17. There is no suggestion in any of the reports of the trial that Shkolnik had ever been in contact, directly or indirectly, with any agent of the Israeli government or of any other government. Nor was there any suggestion that Shkolnik did in fact, at any time, actually transfer, either in writing or orally, any of the information described in paragraph 16 to Israel, or to any representative or agent of the Israeli government, or to any agent of any government. None of the materials seized in the search of Shkolnik's apartment indicated communication with any Israeli agent. (The visiting card of the British engineer, described in paragraph 10, indicated contact

with a person from Britain who was in Vinnitsa for approved commercial reasons, but Shkolnik was not even charged with spying for Britain.) Rather all reports of Shkolnik's conviction clearly indicate that Shkolnik was convicted for intention to transmit certain information to Israel at some time in the future if and when the circumstances permitted it.

18. To establish criminal liability for treasonous acts of espionage, it is necessary, under fundamental principles of Soviet law, to establish that the accused possessed a present intent to complete the criminal act of transmission of the "secrets." The undisputed facts of this case leave no doubt that Shkolnik could not be found to have possessed the requisite present intent.

There is no dispute that at the time that Shkolnik was arrested on July 5, 1972, he had not yet filed an application with the authorities for an exit visa to emigrate to Israel. The *Soviet Weekly* article of April 21, 1973, reported that Shkolnik had "planned to apply to the Soviet authorities for permission to go to Israel. He did not, however, have time to put in an application to leave the U.S.S.R. and only after his arrest were requests certified by Israeli immigration authorities, who sent his name from Israel." But the same report states that Shkolnik had collected information "with a view to selling it to Israeli intelligence when he arrived in Israel." Therefore, it is clear that during the period when Shkolnik was allegedly collecting information in order to transmit when he arrived in Israel, he had done nothing to accomplish the goal of arriving in Israel. Moreover, Shkolnik did not possess the capability of accomplishing that goal; he was dependent upon a decision by the proper authorities as to whether or not he would receive the necessary permission to leave the Soviet Union. But Shkolnik could not in any way control, or even affect, whether or not the decision by the authorities would be to grant him the permission. Thus Shkolnik could not know if he would receive the requisite permission to leave, or if so, when he would receive such permission. His alleged intention to transmit information to Israel, then, was at most a conditional intention which could only become an actual and present intention if and when events outside of his power occurred. Such a conditional intention cannot be the basis of a conviction for treason. Since Shkolnik was convicted of treason at a time when he had no actual and present intention to transmit information to Israel, the verdict cannot be justified.

19. Nor did Shkolnik possess the capability of collecting the information described in paragraph 15. It appears from the reports of the trial that no evidence was adduced to suggest that Shkolnik had collected any of the described information on paper or in any permanent form. The search of his apartment revealed no documentary

evidence of collection of any "secret" information. Yet Shkolnik was charged with "persistently" and "systematically" collecting the information "for several years." It is clear that if Shkolnik did collect the secret information as charged, he collected it only by committing the information to memory, and by storing the details in his mind for a period of at least several years, for the time when he might obtain the possibility of transmitting it to Israel.

20. Information of the sort described in paragraph 15 must necessarily include copious and complex details, both numerical and descriptive, regarding locations, measurements, specifications, and military plans and strategy. It cannot be "systematically" and "persistently" gathered and memorized by a person who does not possess the training and mental skill essential to understanding and absorbing and synthesizing highly technical and strategic planning. Indeed, it would appear that only a person of extraordinary mental powers could perform the feat charged. Despite evidence that Shkolnik read some military and scientific publications, there is no evidence that Shkolnik possessed the technical training and mental skills necessary to permit a person to understand, absorb, and synthesize information of the sort he allegedly collected. On the contrary, every indication is that Shkolnik did not possess the requisite mental skills for such a task. He had no secondary or higher education; he had worked only as a laborer, miner, mechanic, and fitter. Without the availability of the court verdict and decision, it is hard to imagine what evidence could have been received which could establish that Shkolnik had the capability of systematically gathering and committing to memory—and then retaining for some indefinite length of time, at least as long as "several years"—the alleged information. If such evidence was not received, there is not sufficient basis for the verdict against him.

21. Accordingly, based upon the evidence and circumstances known to the undersigned and set forth in paragraphs 16 to 20, the conviction of Shkolnik for treason appears to be unjustifiable.

22. The punishment was excessive in light of the failure of the plan. It is undisputed that no harm was caused to the Soviet Union in this case. Any harm which Shkolnik might have been allegedly planning did not occur; he did not in fact transmit any information of any sort to any representative from Israel or from any other government, nor was he even close to doing so since he had not yet even applied for a visa to emigrate. It is a fundamental principle of Soviet law that the less proximate a criminal act is to the ultimate harm, the lower the punishment should be. Accordingly, the seven-year penalty imposed on Shkolnik in this case should be reduced to reflect the undisputed fact that he did not even come close to perpetrating the ultimate harm he was allegedly planning. This point

is developed in Legal Memorandum IV, which is incorporated here by reference.

23. The verdict against Shkolnik for anti-Soviet agitation and propaganda may be unjustifiable. Criminal liability for anti-Soviet agitation and propaganda requires proof of intent to cause harm to the Soviet Union. The core element of the offense is that the propaganda be circulated "for the purpose of subverting or weakening the Soviet regime or of committing particular, especially dangerous crimes against the state," and also describes as criminal the circulation or possession, with that purpose, of "slanderous fabrications which defame the Soviet state and social system." Without the decision or verdict, the undersigned cannot determine what evidence was relied upon by the military tribunal for its finding that Shkolnik was guilty of anti-Soviet agitation and propaganda. However, according to the petitioner, as is sworn to in the petitioner's affidavits, no expert testimony regarding the anti-Soviet nature of Shkolnik's communications to others was received at the trial. Nor did the search of Shkolnik's apartment disclose documents which would appear to support a verdict of guilty for possession of anti-Soviet propaganda. It is known, however, that evidence regarding Shkolnik's desire to emigrate to Israel was received at the trial. Under fundamental principles of Soviet law, evidence of a desire merely to leave the U.S.S.R. and relocate elsewhere without more cannot be relied on as the sole basis for a finding of intent to cause harm to the Soviet Union. If Shkolnik's desire to emigrate was the only basis for the conviction under Article 62 of the Ukrainian Criminal Code, then it cannot be justified.

24. Denial of Shkolnik's right to counsel of his choice and to a defense. Petitioner swears to certain facts regarding Shkolnik's defense and regarding the lawyer who acted as his defense counsel; and a "statement" sent jointly by the petitioner and by Shkolnik's parents to the Chairman of the Military Tribunal of the Zakarpatsky Military District, and to the Chairman of the Vinnitsa Regional Advocates' Collegiate objecting to the lawyer who acted as Shkolnik's defense counsel. As set forth, therein, and as hereinafter indicated, Shkolnik was deprived of his right to counsel.

25. According to petitioner's affidavit the following events occurred: after Shkolnik's arrest on July 5, 1972, his wife, the petitioner, undertook to obtain legal representation for him. She was informed that she had no choice of counsel since there was only one lawyer in Vinnitsa, Nikolai Davidovich Makarenko, who possessed the necessary permission required by the KGB to undertake to represent her husband. Having no choice, Shkolnik's wife retained Makarenko, but from the very first Makarenko failed to fulfill his duties to provide her husband with proper legal aid.

26. From the beginning, Makarenko considered Shkolnik guilty of the charges against him and refused to defend him on any other ground. Makarenko used every effort to persuade Shkolnik to plead guilty as charged. According to the petitioner, Makarenko informed her husband that he could not avoid the death penalty if he did not plead guilty. At trial, Shkolnik admitted his guilt, but from her conversations with her husband after his trial, when she was permitted to visit her husband in prison, the petitioner learned that Shkolnik's admission of guilt was neither voluntary nor truthful. In any event, under Soviet law a guilty plea, even in open court, is not sufficient in itself to support a judgment of guilty.

27. At the trial, Shkolnik's lawyer called only a very few witnesses on Shkolnik's behalf. The petitioner declares in her affidavit that she knows of other witnesses who would have given testimony on Shkolnik's behalf but were not called by his lawyer. It is clear from these facts that the only lawyer available to Shkolnik—one not of his choice—failed to make use of all means and methods to provide Shkolnik a defense at trial designed to rebut the charges against him.

28. In her affidavit the petitioner further declares the following: after Shkolnik was convicted, the petitioner attempted to ensure that an appeal would be taken on her husband's behalf. When she visited Shkolnik at the Vinnitsa prison, she attempted to discuss his appeal with him but was prevented from doing so by the prison guard in attendance. Makarenko then refused to file the appeal. Therefore, the petitioner retained the services of another lawyer named Sarri, to whom she was referred by the Moscow Collegium. Sarri immediately went to the headquarters of the Military Tribunal at Lvov, studied her husband's case, and received permission to visit him in the Vinnitsa prison. Sarri went to the prison on April 19, 1973, but despite the permission given him by the authorities at Lvov, the prison officials did not permit him to see Shkolnik. While Sarri waited at the prison, Makarenko was called and came to the prison. Makarenko and the prison officials advised Shkolnik that he should not see Sarri and required him to sign a written statement authorizing Makarenko as his lawyer. The obstruction by Makarenko and the prison authorities deprived Shkolnik of the opportunity to meet and communicate with counsel of his family's choice. After Sarri attempted to see Shkolnik, Makarenko did file an appeal which he backdated to a date prior to Sarri's visit. Several days before the cassational appeal, the petitioner went to the Moscow Military Collegium of the Supreme Court and attempted to file a dismissal of Makarenko but was not permitted to do so. Sarri filed a complaint with the authorities in Moscow concerning the obstruction of his attempt to act on behalf of Shkolnik.

29. The facts set forth in paragraphs 24 to 28 constitute clear violations of Soviet criminal procedural law. Under Soviet law, an accused is entitled to counsel of his choice and to be represented by such counsel in his efforts to defend himself against the charges. These principles of law are clear from Chapter 3 of the Code of Criminal Procedure, particularly Articles 46, 48, 50 and 51, and are discussed in more detail in Legal Memorandum I, submitted separately by the undersigned in support of this and other petitions. Article 51 of the Code of Criminal Procedure, entitled *Duties and Rights of Defense Counsel,* provides that "Defense counsel shall be obliged to make use of all means and methods of defense indicated in the law for the purpose of explaining the circumstances tending to acquit the accused or to mitigate his responsibility, and to render the accused necessary legal aid." Shkolnik was not permitted to choose his counsel, either for his trial or for his appeal, and the counsel who represented him failed to fulfill his duties under Article 51 to make use of all means and methods of defense on Shkolnik's behalf. . . .

TELFORD TAYLOR

June 10, 1974   Attorney for Petitioner

ANNEX A

June 13, 1973

TO the Presidium of the Supreme Soviet of the U.S.S.R.

TO the Secretary General of the Central Committee of the CPSU, Brezhnev

COPY TO the Military Board of the Supreme Court of the U.S.S.R.

My husband, Isaac Rafailovich Shkolnik, has been sentenced by the military court of the Cis-Carpathian Military District to ten years imprisonment on the charge of treason to the Fatherland and espionage.

The court recognized that Shkolnik had not been recruited and was not an agent of any intelligence service, that he had not transmitted information to anyone, and that consequently he had not caused any real harm to the country and could not have caused it.

My husband is a technically illiterate man and has no special education. He simply was unable to differentiate what information is important and is a government secret. The information that was in the possession of my husband could have been in the possession of any other person; therefore I am certain that he had not only not caused any harm to the Soviet state, but that he had been unable to do so. This is confirmed by the fact that not a single one of the witnesses who testified against him had been called to answer for making public a state secret; that is, in spite of the examination of the experts which had been carried out, he was not a bearer of secret information.

I have grounds to suppose that the testimony given by my husband was self-slander. It also appeared half a year after the beginning of the investigation. In support of this supposition is the statement by Makarenko to the effect that should Shkolnik be evasive in court, a death sentence would not be excluded.

The testimony might have been the result of exhaustion from the lengthy investigation.

Had he really nurtured some sorts of plans and should his admission be true, then it is an act of repentance and excludes the further realization of these plans. There is no other proof, except his own testimony, in the possession of the court and of the investigation, that he had planned to take this information to Israel. From the fact that his testimony was an act of repentance or of self-slander it proceeds that in the future he will not be a danger to the Soviet state.

All the above stated gives me the right to consider that the conviction of my husband is a tragic misunderstanding, and I beg you to repeal this cruel sentence.

FEIGA SHKOLNIK

ANNEX B

TO the Procurator General of the U.S.S.R., Rudenko
TO the committee of Jurists-democrats in Brussels
FROM Feiga Moiseevna Shkolnik, Vinnitsa, Kosmonavtov St. 14, apt. 19, tel. 4-37-61

PETITION

On July 5, 1972, my husband, Isaac Rafailovich Shkolnik, born in 1936, was arrested. During his arrest a search was made of our apartment. The purpose of the search was to find leaflets and other documents. Nothing of the sort and nothing illegal from the point of view of Soviet laws was found. It is already seven months that he is under arrest. At first he was charged in accordance with Statute 187 of the Criminal Code of the Ukrainian S.S.R. (point 190 of the Code of the R.S.F.S.R.) Statute 52(70). At present, the investigator informed me that against my husband there is a new charge in accordance with Statute 56(64)—treason to the Fatherland. I don't know how the investigation reached such a terrible accusation, but I am certain that my husband did not and could not commit an act that could be regarded as treason to the Fatherland. He is blamed for his good knowledge of English and his acquaintance with foreigners, who came to our country as tourists or on missions. He always met openly with them, in places where there were many people, in our home, at the birthday party for our daughter. At these meetings many of our acquaintances and relatives were always present. He is also blamed for visiting expositions organized by foreign states in our country, such as "Popular Education in the U.S.A.," "Communication Media in the U.S.A.," etc. Why then had these expositions been organized at the time?

I know that my husband had done honest work all his life: he worked as a laborer, a miner, on factory building sites, and as a mechanic. He was a simple laborer and had no access to important information. His only guilt consists of his desire to go to the state of Israel, considering that this is the historical homeland of the Jews, and consequently his homeland, too.

It is only the lack of an affidavit that had prevented him from applying for emigration. He never concealed from anyone his desire to go to Israel. This was known by his comrades and by his relatives and at his place of employment. He did not consider this a crime.

I beg you to make an investigation in the matter and not to allow that such a terrible and unjust charge be brought against him.

FEIGA SHKOLNIK—the wife of Isaac Shkolnik
Vinnitsa, 4.2.73

ANNEX C

TO the chairman of the Military Collegium of the Supreme Court of U.S.S.R.
the Chairman of the Military Tribunal of the Zakarpatsky Military District
COPY to the Chairman of the Vinnitsa Regional Advocates Collegiate
FROM the relatives of the convicted I. R. Shkolnik: F. M. Shkolnik, R. M. Shkolnik, R. N. Shkolnik.

STATEMENT

We have engaged advocate Makarenko to act as the defense counsel of I. R. Shkolnik in the court of first instance. Following his refusal to lodge the cassation complaint and the fact that he wrote it only after we had sent telegrams to the Minister of Justice of Ukrainian S.S.R., the Minister of Justice of U.S.S.R., and the Chairman of the Supreme Court of U.S.S.R., in which we asked that he should be made to lodge the complaint, and also because of the fact that the actions of Makarenko aroused our doubts as to his conscientiousness, we had officially refused his services in the future and asked him not to visit I. R. Shkolnik.

We had applied to the Moscow Advocates Collegium with a request to appoint an advocate to act as defense counsel in the Military Collegiate of the Supreme Court. We did so to avoid any local influences on the defense counsel because we were doubtful as to the correctness of advocate Makarenko's actions.

The advocate, who came from Moscow, saw the materials of the case and, having received official permission for a visit, came to Vinnitsa on the 16th of April 1973. We accompanied him to the prison. He went inside and then returned saying that the director of the prison did not allow the visit and asked him to come after 12:00 as he allegedly must find out who will defend Shkolnik: Makarenko or this advocate.

We went to the Advocates Collegium and found that despite our requests not to visit with Shkolnik, Makarenko went to the prison to see him. The advocate from Moscow came to the prison after 12:00 in the afternoon and came out saying that according to the statement by the prison's director, Shkolnik had allegedly written a statement saying that he wants Makarenko to act as his defense counsel and that he refuses the services of any other advocate.

The above-mentioned facts had aroused our doubts. Why had our husband and son, not having seen and spoken to the advocate from Moscow, refused the services of any other advocate apart from Makarenko? Why is advocate Makarenko, in whom we had no trust and whose services we had refused, insisting on leading the defense in the future? Why had the director of the prison refused the advocate from Moscow the permission for a visit and asked him to come back after 12:00? And in the meantime he had allowed advocate Makarenko to visit Shkolnik and to obtain the statement, according to his words, from Shkolnik? Why did not the director of the prison, who was obliged by law to do so, allow the advocate from Moscow to visit Shkolnik, as the advocate had an official permission issued by the Military Tribunal, and base his refusal on Shkolnik's statement?

We think that the director of the prison was obliged to allow the advocate from Moscow to visit Shkolnik, and Shkolnik if he really wanted, could himself have said that he refused the services of the advocate from Moscow, preferring advocate Makarenko.

Objectively it transpires that Shkolnik, who is the son of one of us and the husband of another, is being hidden and is not being given the opportunity to see anyone except advocate Makarenko, whom we do not trust. The advocate from Moscow, who had an assignment to lead Shkolnik's defense, was not allowed to meet him, and Makarenko, who did not have an assignment to lead the defense in the cassation instance, was allowed to do so.

We doubt that Shkolnik's statement, to which the director of the prison referred, was given voluntarily, and we are beginning to doubt the correctness of the actions of the prison administration and of advocate Makarenko. We have the impression that some sort of pressure is being exerted on Shkolnik and because of this the advocate engaged by us was not allowed to meet him. We think so also because of the fact that during our meeting with Shkolnik we were not allowed to speak to him about the cassation and about the invitation of another advocate. The prison officials who were present during our meeting said that if we talked about it they would discontinue the meeting.

Both we and the advocate chosen by us were deprived of the opportunity to hear personally from Shkolnik that he had chosen Makarenko to act as his defense counsel and refused anyone else, and the reasons for this. We are being compelled to refer to the statements received with Makarenko's participation.

The advocate from Moscow informed us that he was going back to Moscow because he was not allowed to meet with Shkolnik and he was told that Shkolnik had chosen Makarenko as his defense counsel.

We categorically object to Makarenko's leading the defense. We will not register an agreement with him, and we think that from the moral point of view he had no right to lead the defense. We insist that the advocate of the Moscow Collegiate should be acting as the defense counsel.

FEIGA SHKOLNIK
R. M. SHKOLNIK
R. N. SHKOLNIK

C. Legal Memorandums

LEGAL MEMORANDUM I
Right to a Defense in Soviet Law

1. One of the most basic principles of Soviet criminal procedure is that the defendant is entitled to a defense. This provision is guaranteed by Article 111 of the Constitution of the U.S.S.R. and by Article 19, Code of Criminal Procedure (C.C.P.), R.S.F.S.R. Soviet writers, led by V. I. Lenin, have always stressed that the right to a defense is one of the basic principles of Soviet procedure. A partial list of authorities stressing the centrality of the right to a defense includes the following: Soviet writings: *Osnovy sovetskogo gosudarstvennogo stroitelstva i prava* (Moscow, 1965), pp. 379–380 (at 379: "Vazhnym konstitucionnym principom pravosudiia v SSSR iavliaetsia obespecheniie obvinaemomu prava na zashchitu."); *Rol' V. L. Lenina v stanovlenii i razvitii sovetskogo zakonodatelstva* (Moscow, 1969), pp. 453–454; *Nauchno-prakticheskii kommentarii upk RSFSR* (Moscow, 1970), comm. to Article 19; *Sovetskii advokat* (Moscow, 1968), pp. 3–4; *Advokatura v SSSR* (Moscow, 1971), pp. 6–7; *Zashchitnik v sovetskom sude* (Moscow, 1960), pp. 8–9.

2. The right to a defense is a general concept that is expressed in a number of specific, more detailed rules. One of these specific manifestations of the constitutional right to a defense is, as provided in Article 48, C.C.P., R.S.F.S.R., the right of the defendant to choose his own lawyer. In a decision rendered December 17, 1971, the Supreme Court of the U.S.S.R. (panel for criminal cases) held that "depriving the defendant of the possibility of commissioning a lawyer according to his own choice required reversal of the conviction." Furthermore, Soviet legislation consistently stresses the broad range of persons from whom the defendant may select a lawyer according to his personal wishes. See Article 47, C.C.P., R.S.F.S.R., Article 22, Principles U.S.S.R. There is no reference in any of the statutory material, in any of the published regulations, or in any of the official commentaries, to limitations on the range of lawyers who are permitted to appear in "special cases."

3. Materials from the record, supporting affidavits of observers, and petitions show that, in the cases under consideration, the right to an effective defense was abridged in several respects. Some of these errors were in violation of specific provisions of the Code of Criminal Procedure or the Criminal Code; all of them directly or indirectly contributed to a denial of the constitutional right to a defense. The errors fall into the following categories:

—Refusal to permit a defendant to be represented by the counsel of his choice;
—Assignment of counsel to a defendant who preferred a different counsel;
—Refusal to permit a defendant to discharge and replace an unsatisfactory counsel;
—Unjustified failure to file cassation appeals;
—Unjustified failure to make a vigorous defense;
—Refusal to permit counsel to interview his client;
—Refusal to permit counsel to take notes of the interview with his client;
—Refusal to permit counsel to take with him his notes on materials of the case;
—Unjustified refusal to call witnesses at defendant's request;
—Suppression or interruption of testimony that would have been favorable to the defense.

In the cases under consideration, the defendants were not allowed to exercise their constitutional right to select a lawyer according to their preferences. In several situations, the defendant was forced to accept a lawyer who had a special permit (*dopusk*) but was not the lawyer of his preference. See the affidavits of Shkolnik and Grilius.

4. Limiting the choice of counsel to lawyers officially approved resulted in numerous instances in which the defendant was denied the services of a lawyer willing to perform the function of a defense counsel. That function, as defined by Article 23, Principles U.S.S.R., is "to take all indicated means and methods of defense in the interest of clarifying the circumstances tending to exculpate the defendant or to reduce his responsibility or to render him all necessary legal assistance." In certain respects, several of the lawyers whom the defendants were obliged to retain failed to fulfill this obligation. In several instances they refused to file cassational appeals. See the affidavit of Shkolnik. In other instances, the lawyers refused to defend their clients against the charges levied against them. According to G. P. Sarkisjanets, the author of *Defense Counsel in the Criminal Process* (Tashkent, 1971), Article 249, C.C.P., R.S.F.S.R., requires that the defense counsel conduct himself in a manner that assists, rather than harms, his client (see page 25). In the cases dis-

cussed above, it is clear that the defense counsel did not act in the interest of their clients; as a result, *there was direct violation of Article 249, C.C.P.,* and a violation also of the constitutional right (Article 111) to a defense.

5. The constitutional right to a defense also means that state officials should not interfere with the lawyer's performance of his statutory duty. According to Article 51, C.C.P., R.S.F.S.R., the defense counsel has a right to an interview with his client. This right was not respected in the Shkolnik case. With regard to the case of L. Korenblit, defense counsel was allowed to meet with the accused, but he was not allowed to take notes during the interview. There were other instances in which defense counsel were allowed to take notes at the time they examined the materials of the case, but they were not allowed to remove these notes from the room. This prohibition was in violation of Article 202, C.C.P., R.S.F.S.R., which grants defense counsel the right to "take notes on all necessary information" from the file of the case. These incidents all represent violations of specific rules; in addition, and more significantly, they represent impediments to the realization of the defendants' constitutional right to a defense.

6. One of the essential features of the constitutional right to a defense is the defendant's right to reject his defense counsel at any time and to proceed, if he should wish, on his own. See Article 50, C.C.P., R.S.F.S.R. This right was violated in the Shkolnik case, for when the accused became dissatisfied with his defense counsel, he was not allowed to reject that counsel and replace him with another. The right guaranteed in Article 50 was also violated in the case of Butman, who as a professionally trained jurist preferred to undertake his own defense. There were no circumstances suggesting that Butman was less than fully qualified to undertake his defense. He had a clear statutory right to do so; see point 5 in the commentary to Article 50, *Scientific-Practical Commentary to C.C.P., R.S.F.S.R.* (1971), at page 78. Denying Butman his right to defend himself was a violation of Article 50 and, furthermore, a violation of Butman's constitutional right to a defense.

7. The most essential aspect of a constitutional right to a defense is the right to present evidence at trial. See Articles 46 and 51, C.C.P., R.S.F.S.R. There are numerous instances in which defendants requested that witnesses be called on their behalf and the requests were denied. See the affidavit in the case of Knokh. These were cases in which the defendants were not allowed to call *any witnesses whatever* in their behalf. Accordingly, it cannot be contended that the evidence to be given by them would have been duplicative or correlative, for *no* prior testimony had been given by witnesses in behalf of the defendant. The witnesses whose testimony

the defendants sought unsuccessfully were the only means by which the defendants could present the evidence which they wished the court to consider. Denying the request for the appearance of witnesses denied the right to present evidence under Articles 46 and 51, C.C.P., R.S.F.S.R.

8. Another aspect of the right to present evidence, as guaranteed under Articles 46 and 51, C.C.P., R.S.F.S.R., is the right to have evidence favorable to the defense considered at trial. Yet there are repeated instances in which witnesses, when they began to testify in a way that was favorable to the defense, were interrupted. This happened most markedly in the case of Kaminsky, in which a witness for the defense was interrupted as soon as he began to present evidence favorable to the accused. That this happened at the trial is supported by two eyewitness accounts; see the affidavits of Kaminsky and Knokh. That this was a repeated occurrence in those trials is supported by the affidavits of Vudka and Grilius as to similar incidents in the trial in Ryazan in February 1970. The most egregious incident violating the right to a defense occurred when a prosecution witness, M. Korenblit, was interrupted and removed from the courtroom. He was not allowed to remain for examination by the defense counsel and other participants in the trial. By forcibly removing him from the room the court thus violated the established procedure for the hearing of testimony; see Article 283, C.C.P., R.S.F.S.R., which prescribes that the witness must be examined by all of the participants in the criminal trial. The peremptory and unjustified interruption of witnesses, even of witnesses called by the prosecution, violated the right of the defendant to present evidence under Articles 46 and 51, C.C.P., R.S.F.S.R., and, more significantly, violated the defendant's constitutional right to a defense.

10 June 1974   /s/ TELFORD TAYLOR

LEGAL MEMORANDUM II

> *Procedures Used to Ascertain Anti-Soviet Character of Seized Literature*
>
> *Section 70, Criminal Code, R.S.F.S.R., and the use of Expert Witnesses**

I. The purpose of this memorandum is to assess the legality of the procedures by which various items of literature were found to fit

* The following abbreviations are used in the memorandum:
CC RSFSR: *Ugolovnyj Kodsk RSFSR* (Criminal Code of R.S.F.S.R.)
CCP RSFSR: *Ugolovnyj—protsessual'nyj Kodeks* RSFSR (Code of Criminal Procedure of R.S.F.S.R.)

the definition prescribed in Section 70, Criminal Code, R.S.F.S.R. The first section discusses the legal context in which the question arises.

1. Convictions under §70, CC RSFSR were a central feature of the prosecutions against virtually all the defendants represented by the present petitioners. Conviction under §70 provided the focus for the trials in Ryazan in February 1970 (against Grilius, Vudka, and others), in Leningrad in December 1970 (against Dymshitz, Kuznetsov, and others) in Leningrad in May 1971 (Butman, Korenblit, and others), in Kishinev in June 1970 (Chernoglaz and others), and in Leningrad in October 1971 (against Azernikov).

2. The distribution of literature in violation of §70 provided an important part of the Procuracy's proof of treason (§64, CC RSFSR), in both of the Leningrad trials. Section 64 provides that flight abroad constitutes treason; but to distinguish the especially grave crime of treason from the less serious crime of illegally leaving the U.S.S.R. (§83, CC RSFSR), the statute itself and the *Commentary to the Criminal Code* (1971) make it clear that treason presupposes leaving the country with the intent of harming "the governmental, independence, the territorial integrity of the U.S.S.R." (*Commentary,* p. 158). To prove this additional anti-Soviet intent, above and beyond the intent to leave the country, the prosecution in the Leningrad trials relied heavily on the hostility to the Soviet Union that supposedly was implicit in distributing literature in violation of §70. That this was an indispensable part of the proof of the intent is established by the Decision of the Supreme Court, U.S.S.R., December 31, 1970, which states: "The fact that the convicted defendants had treasonable aims is confirmed also by the fact that the majority of them (Kuznetsov, Mendelevich, I. Zalmanson, Altman, Knokh) systematically engaged in preparing and duplication of literature hostile to the Soviet order . . ." (page 16 of English translation).

3. If the distribution of literature in violation of §70 constitutes an indispensable element in providing the foundation for treason under §64, it is especially important that the proof of the convictions under §70 conform to the principles of socialist legality. If the convictions under §70 are not legally valid, it follows that the convictions of Dymshitz, Kuznetsov, Mendelevich, Knokh, Altman, the Zalmansons, Butman, and Korenblit under §64 are based on an invalid legal foundation.

Principles CC: *Osnovy ugolovnogo zakonadetel'stvo* U.S.S.R. (Basic Principles of Criminal Legislation for the U.S.S.R.)

Principles CCP: *Osnovy ugolovnogo cudoproisvodstva* C.C.C.P. (Basic Principles of Criminal Procedure for the U.S.S.R.)

4. The elements of §70, as applied to cases represented in this petition, are:

1. the objective element: that the defendant possess, reproduce, or distribute literature "discrediting the Soviet governmental or social order";

2. the subjective element: that this act of possession, reproduction or distribution be done with the "aim of harming or weakening the Soviet regime."

5. Whether or not items of literature "discredit the governmental or social order" is a question to be resolved under Soviet law. This memorandum is submitted with full respect for the capacity of the Soviet courts to determine, upon the full and complete evaluation of the evidence, whether specific items of literature possess the tendencies specified under §70.

6. The question of the intent required under §70 is discussed in Section IV of this memorandum. Section II of this memorandum has the limited objective of assessing the *procedure* by which various items of literature were found to meet the *objective criteria* of §70, CC RSFSR.

II. The required procedures for establishing that particular items of literature meet the objective standard of "discrediting the Soviet governmental or social order" were not followed.

1. The Criminal Code defines the kind of literature that is covered by §70. Thus, the quality of the literature is an element of the *sostav*. The most elementary principle of socialist legality is that all elements of the *sostav* must be proven at the trial. See §68 CCP, RSFSR.

2. In all of the cases under consideration, the court concluded in its judgment that the literature, possessed or distributed, was "anti-Soviet." It is a basic rule of Soviet criminal procedure that all judgments must be legally and factually well-founded (§43, Principles CCP; §301, CCP RSFSR). It is also a basic rule that the court must account for its conclusion on the basis of evidence heard at trial (§43, Principles CCP; §301, CCP RSFSR).

3. It is also basic that Soviet courts may not base their judgments on the basis of presuppositions or presumptions (§43, Principles CCP). See also the Decree of the Plenum of the Supreme Court, June 30, 1969 (No. 4).

4. How did the courts in the trials involving Article 70 conclude that the various items of literature "discredited the Soviet governmental and social order"? In none of the trial hearings here in question was there any evidence offered in court to show that the litera-

ture had this particular quality. No experts or other influences were called by the prosecution for this purpose. When various defendants tried to assert that the literature was not anti-Soviet in character, the trial judges interrupted them and prevented them from testifying. For documentation of these facts, see the attached affidavits of Sonia Druk, Polina Korenblit, Levit, Vudka, Pinchos Knokh, and Grilius (P–1). All of these affiants were eyewitnesses to the trials. They all testify to a common pattern. The pattern is that no evidence was introduced to prove that the literature in question met the statutory definition of "discrediting the Soviet governmental or social order."

5. That there was no evidence offered at trial does not mean that the trial judges in these cases had no expert advice on the status of the literature. In two of these cases, one or more of the defendants saw that the case file contained an expert analysis of the status of the literature. The protocol (variously designated by the name of the organization that was thought to have prepared it, as *Glavlit* or *Oblit*) was examined by several defendants in the course of examining the files in their case at the end of the preliminary investigation. See the affidavit of Levit, who swore to having seen such protocols identifying the literature in their case as "anti-Soviet." It appears altogether probable that this was the situation in all of petitioner's cases involving Article 70.

6. It follows that the literature in these cases was identified as "anti-Soviet" not through testimony or other factual evidence, but either on the basis of a "presupposition" or on the basis of the expert's protocol in the file of the case. Both of these possibilities represent a violation of Soviet law. The reliance on a presupposition that the literature was anti-Soviet violates §43, Principles CCP. And if the trial courts relied on the *Glavlit* protocols, there were violations of numerous provisions of Soviet criminal procedure, for the reasons set forth in the following section.

III. Violations of the Codes of Criminal Procedures

1. The discussion in this memorandum does not touch the question whether the reports submitted by *Glavlit* contained an accurate and fair analysis of the literature in question. In this kind of case, expert testimony is appropriate; see §78, CCP RSFSR.

2. If the protocols submitted by *Glavlit* and contained in the files of the cases were to be used as evidence against him, it was the duty of the trial judge to read the protocols publicly at the trials (§240, CCP RSFSR; §37, Principles CCP). The failure to read the protocols violated these provisions and thereby violated the principles of "oral review" of the evidence—a principle that Professor Strogovich identifies as one of the absolute principles of Soviet criminal pro-

cedure. Professor Strogovich says that other principles may admit of exceptions and limitations, but not the principle of "oral review" at trial (M. Strogovich, *Kurs Sovetskogo Protsessa,* vol. I, p. 165 [1968]). This principle required that all the *Glavlit* protocols contained in the case file be read publicly at the trials. This was not done in any of the trials herein discussed.

3. So far as these judgments were based on protocols *not* read at trial, the judgments also violated §301, CCP RSFSR, §43, Principles CCP. The judgment that the literature "discredited the Soviet governmental or social order" was based on materials "not reviewed at trial"; thus the judgments were not well-founded, as required by §301, CCP RSFSR.

4. This procedure stands in sharp contrast to the information concerning the procedure followed in the case against Daniel in 1966. There, according to accounts of that trial, the prosecutor repeatedly referred to *Glavlit*'s findings and gave the defendants some opportunity to respond to these findings. Also, in this trial, the trial Judge L. N. Smirnov advised the defense counsel that two of the experts were not present and asked whether they nevertheless wished to proceed. The literary expert Alexander Dymshitz was present at the trial, and all agreed to proceed under these circumstances. The assessment of *Glavlit* was disclosed and debated. Expert witnesses were present at the trial. Thus, there may have been in the language of §20, CCP, RSFSR, a "comprehensive, full, and objective" inquiry whether the works of Sinjavsky and Daniel conformed to the objective standard of §70.

5. In the trial of the petitioners, the courts failed to meet the standard of legality set by the trial of Sinjavsky and Daniel. A decree of the Supreme Court of the U.S.S.R. explains this pattern of failing to conform to socialist legality in the field of expert witnesses. *Postanovlenie No. 1,* issued by the Plenum of the Supreme Court of the U.S.S.R., March 16, 1971, calls on trial judges to correct their excessive reliance on the conclusions offered by experts. Point 9 of the *Postanovlenie* lays down the rule that the courts must review at trial all the evidence bearing on the expert's conclusion. Merely relying on an expert's conclusion as to the status of suspected literature, violates this command of the Supreme Court.

6. In a subsequent article, published in the *Bulleten' Verkhovnogo Suda* (1971), No. 3, p. 37, the commentator documents the systematic abuses that led to the *Postanovlenie* of March 16, 1971. It is clear from this report that in the period preceding the decree, namely in the years 1970 and early 1971, the trial courts were relying unduly on expert conclusions. They were basing their judgments on expert conclusions without reviewing the matters fully at trial as required by §§20, 240 and 301, CCP RSFSR. They were, in short,

engaged in the kind of abuse that occurred in the period of time in which petitioners' trials took place.

7. It was clearly in the interests of socialist legality to correct this pattern of abuse and to seek to restore the proper role of trial judges in deciding whether the expert's conclusion is sound. The *Postanovlenie* of March 16, 1971, is intended to accomplish this for future cases. In a case under §70, CC RSFSR, the trial judge should seek the advice of experts, as did Judge Smirnov in the trial of Sinjavsky and Daniel. The experts' conclusion should be openly presented at trial, as is required by the principle of §240, CC RSFSR. To place reliance on a secret, undisclosed, unexamined conclusion of an expert, as was done in the cases with which we are concerned here, is a violation of socialist legality.

IV. There was no proof that the allegedly anti-Soviet literature was reproduced or distributed with the intent required for conviction under §70, CC RSFSR.

1. According to the language of the statute, the offense specified in §70, CC RSFSR, presupposes an intent to "subvert or weaken the Soviet regime." According to the official commentary published in 1971, this intent requires that the defendant be aware of the anti-Soviet character of the literature that he possesses, reproduces, or distributes. See *Sovetskoe Ugolovnoe Pravo: Osobennaja Chast'* (1971), at p. 47: The intent required under §70 is different from that required under §75, CC RSFSR, which merely requires that a person disclosing a governmental secret intend to disclose information constituting a governmental secret. See *Kommentarij k Ugolovnomu Kodeksu* (1971), at p. 173. Implicitly, it is not necessary under §75 that the actor be aware that the information amounts to a governmental secret. Yet, as indicated above, the intent required *under §70* must encompass knowledge of the anti-Soviet character of the literature as well as the intent to possess, reproduce, or distribute such literature with the purpose of weakening the Soviet state.

2. The judgments in these trials fail to address themselves to the subjective element of §70, CC RSFSR. There appears to be no finding made on the intent required for commission of the offense. As a result, the judgments in these cases cannot be regarded as well-founded and legally sound, as required by §301, CCP RSFSR.

3. On the basis of numerous eyewitness reports of the trials, a consistent pattern emerges. The court made no effort to inquire into the objective element. For proof of this pattern, see the attached affidavits, listed above in point II, 3. It was simply assumed that the literature was possessed, reproduced, or distributed both (1) with knowledge of the alleged anti-Soviet character of this

literature, and (2) with the intent "to subvert or weaken the Soviet regime." In assuming this intent—an element that should have been proved at trial—the courts in all these convictions violated §43, Principles CCP, which prohibits rendering judgments on the basis of presuppositions or presumptions.

4. It would be erroneous to argue that the required intent may be inferred from the mere fact that literature was possessed, reproduced, or distributed. If there were anti-Soviet passages in these works, they were passages included among numerous other portions, that did not pertain to any questions related to the Soviet regime. None of the judgments specified what particular passages were anti-Soviet in character. It is apparent that much, if not most, of the literature was intended to convey information about the Jewish religion and nationality. The presence of some anti-Soviet passage would not, accordingly, adequately support a finding that the defendants' motives in distributing such literature were anti-Soviet rather than national or religious.

5. Even if some of the defendants admitted at trial that the literature was anti-Soviet, this admission would not be sufficient to prove their intent as required under §70. According to V. Kaminsky *Pokasanija obvinjaemogo v sovetskom ugolovnom prave* (1960), at p. 79, the admission of the defendant should provide a basis for an inference of fact only if corroborated by objective facts. There were no objective facts in any of the petitioners' cases indicating that they knew that the literature was anti-Soviet. Further, the admissions at trial were a response to the influence of the investigation and the proceedings before the court. They provide no evidence of what their consciousness was before they were exposed to the criminal proceedings. Therefore, these admissions at trial should not be accepted as compliance with the clear command of the law that all elements of the crime be established at trial.

V. The reliance on expert witnesses violated several specific provisions of the CCP designed to guarantee the suspect's right to a defense.

1. There is clear evidence that the investigators in these cases relied on the expert advice of *Glavlit* in concluding that the literature was anti-Soviet. By invoking expert testimony, the prosecutor came under the obligations specified in §184, CCP RSFSR. In particular, the investigator was obligated to advise the suspect of his rights under §185. This was not done in the case of Victor Boguslavsky. When the accused Boguslavsky attempted to exercise his right under §185 to request an additional expert on the question of whether the literature was anti-Soviet, the investigator refused to consider the request. There is no evidence that in any of these cases, the investi-

gator advised the accused of his rights under §185 and no evidence that any of the accused were permitted to exercise any of these well-defined rights.

VI. Summary

On the basis of the foregoing analysis, it is submitted that the procedures followed in proving charges under §70, CC RSFSR, violated basic rules governing the use of expert witnesses. The trials should be reopened in order to comply with the proper procedures for naming experts (§§184 and 185, CCP RSFSR) and for the proper procedures for relying on an expert's conclusion (§37, Principles CCP: §240, §301, CCP RSFSR). In view of the link between proof under §70 and conviction under §64, it is respectfully submitted that, pending the resolution of the disputed status of the conviction under §70, the Procuracy should also regard the conviction under §64 as disputed, and consider reclassifying these convictions under §83, CC RSFSR.

LEGAL MEMORANDUM III

Conditions of Confinement

Introduction

Civilized nations recognize that certain principles of equity and humanity restrict their freedom to punish convicted criminals. Thus, Soviet law includes a number of rights designed to safeguard prisoners from discriminatory or unduly severe deprivations.

But in dealing with large numbers of prison inmates and officials, deviations from the norm are inevitable. Oversights do occur; some administrators may abuse their discretion. To correct such abuses, Soviet law empowers the Procurator General of the U.S.S.R. to maintain supervision of the conditions of prisoner confinement and to take necessary corrective action by directives to the prison or corrective-labor-colony authorities.[1]

According to the affidavits submitted by former prisoners and by the petitioners in these cases, in certain respects the treatment accorded the convicted persons in these cases has not conformed to the requirements of the law, as described and discussed in this memorandum.

I. ENDANGERMENT OF HEALTH

Soviet law is particularly concerned with protecting the health and well-being of inmates. The execution of judicial sentences may not have as its goal the infliction of physical suffering.[2] Thus, prison authorities are required to consider the physical capabilities of inmates in determining their work assignments.[3] Medical institutions at places of confinement are required to render the inmate all types of qualified aid. Similarly, inmates are entitled to receive sufficient food to ensure physical well-being.[4]

A number of the convicted persons involved in these petitions have not enjoyed the full measure of protection guaranteed by Soviet Law. Shkolnik[5] and Mendelevich[6] have been given assignments which are inherently dangerous. Furthermore, in Mendelevich's case,[7] as well as that of Yagman[8] and Markman,[9] work assignments and extreme weather conditions at their camps are aggravating pre-existing ailments.[10] Unrealistic work quotas have been set,[11] which cause needless physical suffering[12] and may result in violations of the eight-hour maximum workday.[13] Mendelevich has been denied necessary medication.[14]

Insufficient food has been provided to many of the prisoners, including Mendelevich,[15] Butman, Yagman, Vudka, and Azernikov.[16] Similarly, inadequate clothing has been provided to many of these same individuals.[17]

Furthermore, some of the affidavits suggest that the physical condition of certain prisoners is such that they may be entitled to relief from serving the remainder of their sentences pursuant to Article 362 or 365 of the R.S.F.S.R. Code of Criminal Procedure. We especially ask that appropriate proceedings be instituted for prisoners Silva Zalmanson, Josif Mendelevich, and Vladimir Markman to determine if such relief is appropriate.

II. DEGRADATION OF HUMAN DIGNITY

Under Soviet law, the execution of corrective sentences may not have as its goal the degradation of human dignity.[18] Anti-Semitism, which degrades both the oppressed and the oppressor, in all of its manifestations has long been illegal in the Soviet Union. Previous law contained specific strictures against this pernicious practice. Currently, the Constitution of the U.S.S.R.[19] and the various republics[20] forbid any direct or indirect restrictions of rights on account of race or nationality. Additionally, the Basic Principles of Legislation Pertaining to Correctional Labor of the U.S.S.R. and the Union Republics require that all prisoners, irrespective of race, religion, or nationality, be regarded equally in the eyes of the law.[21]

Despite the requirements of law, it appears that Jewish prisoners have been exposed to flagrant anti-Semitism in their places of confinement. Prisoners, such as Dymshitz, are routinely confined with and sometimes supervised by[22] former Nazis who remain incorrigible anti-Semites.

As a result the Jewish prisoners have been subjected to verbal and physical abuse in contravention of law. Nazi supervisors have established discriminatory and unrealistic work quotas for their Jewish victims.[23] The authorities, responsible for the administration of detention camps in consonance with socialist legality, have permitted the occurrence and recurrence of these outrages.[24] Indeed, certain prison guards have actually encouraged this despicable behavior.[25] In fact, it appears that the Nazis, most of whom were serving sentences for murder,[26] were routinely given preferential treatment over Jewish prisoners, both with regard to type and amount of work,[27] and with respect to special privileges.[28]

It is doubtful whether giving any prisoners authority over others for disciplinary purposes is legitimate.[29] In any event, prisoners who abuse their authority should have that authority revoked. Prisoners involved in instances of anti-Semitism should be punished and, in appropriate instances, isolated from contact with Jewish prisoners. Guards who permit and foster anti-Semitism should be disciplined. And prison authorities must be held accountable for the prevention of anti-Semitism within their camps. Additionally, we request the Procurator General to take all further action necessary to prevent such degradation of human dignity in the labor camps.

III. ILLEGAL PUNISHMENT

A. *Specification of Rights*

The Corrective Labor Code of the R.S.F.S.R. and the Basic Principles of Legislation Pertaining to Correctional Labor of the U.S.S.R. and the Union Republics provide prisoners with varying rights and privileges depending upon the liberality of the regime to which they have been sentenced. Even those prisoners who have committed the most serious offenses against the social order are not bereft of the protection of law. Thus, even prisoners serving under a special regime are entitled to certain privileges which may not be suspended without just cause.

For example, prisoners are entitled to send out specified numbers of letters every month[30] and to receive an unlimited number.[31] Correspondence must be forwarded by prison authorities, after permissible censorship,[32] within three days of receipt.[33] Convicts have the right to receive parcels from friends and relatives of a weight and number determined by law.[34]

Of course, convicts may be deprived of these privileges for breaches of law and regulation.[35] Additionally, they may be sentenced to punishment cells for aggravated offenses.[36]

However, the prisoners may not be punished if they have not violated the law. Moreover, these penalties must be imposed in accordance with proper legal procedure. Some of the convicted persons have been punished for conduct which is not an offense under Soviet law, and have not been accorded their procedural rights.[37]

B. *Religion*

Freedom of religious worship is guaranteed both by the Constitution of the U.S.S.R.[38] and by the constitutions of the various republics.[39] In fact, it is a violation of the Criminal Code to interfere with the practice of religious rituals which do not disturb the public order.[40] There is no specific limitation upon religious freedom in any known criminal legislation. The Corrective Labor Code of the R.S.F.S.R. describes in detail those deprivations which may legally be inflicted upon prisoners.[41] One may thus infer from the absence of religious restrictions that no such restrictions are permissible which are not reasonably related to the new form of prison administration. Neither is there any question of religious activity on the part of the prisoner that would entail criminal or administrative responsibility.

Additionally, it should be noted that as a member of the United Nations Economic and Social Council, the Soviet Union, on July 31, 1957, voted in favor of the Standard Minimum Rules for the Treatment of Prisoners. Rules 41 and 42 of this document reflect a general policy that prisoners should be afforded an opportunity to practice their religion to the extent that no interference with prison discipline results.

Yet despite these guarantees of religious freedom, Jewish prisoners have been punished for practicing their faith. Thus, Josif Mendelevich is not permitted to engage in prayer, to keep prayer books, nor to wear a hat in accordance with his religious beliefs.[42] Nor is he permitted to observe his Sabbath as a day of rest,[43] even though the Corrective Labor Code of the R.S.F.S.R. requires that prisoners be provided with one day of rest out of seven.[44] Shimon Grilius was not permitted to keep a beard in conformance with his religious belief.[45] In fact, he was severely punished for his insistence upon maintaining this religious requirement even though his right to do so is protected under Soviet law. Similarly, the Vudkas have been subjected to adverse discriminations and penalties as a result of their assertion of their legitimate right to practice their religion.[46] Moreover, the authorities have not assisted the prisoners to maintain their religious dietary requirements while in prison.[47] Consequently, needless physical suffering has been inflicted upon the prisoners in contravention of Soviet law.[48]

C. *Political Lectures*

While prisoners may be encouraged to participate in political education classes,[49] authorities are forbidden to "consider it obligatory for an inmate to engage actively in political measures conducted by the administration or to attend political activities."[50]

Yet Josif Mendelevich, who for religious reasons refused to attend indoctrination classes, has been placed in a punishment cell on restricted diet for this legitimate refusal.[51] Similarly, Hillel Butman was deprived of his right to a visit from his wife because of his alleged refusal to attend certain political activities.[52]

These punishments are clearly illegal and we appeal to the Procurator General to make sure that they do not recur.

D. *Arbitrary or Discriminatory Punishments*

Equally disturbing as the punishments for illegal reasons are those deprivations which have been inflicted for no apparent reason whatsoever. In view of the fact that Jewish prisoners have been singled out for these arbitrary penalties, it appears that a discriminatory pattern has manifested itself in the administration of the corrective labor camps.

For example, prisoners at Potma, including Knokh, Mendelevich, Yagman, and Markman have not received numerous letters addressed to them by their friends and family.[53] In desperation, these prisoners have refused to write to their families in the hope of remedying this situation. Similarly, Dymshitz has had letters he was writing to his family confiscated for no apparent reason.[54] Yagman and Grilius have had their right to receive parcels arbitrarily abrogated.[55] In Grilius's case, a correctly addressed parcel was returned to the sender with the notation "address unknown."[56] Yagman was arbitrarily deprived of his right to a visit from his family.[57] Azernikov had an item he legally bought confiscated from him for no apparent reason.[58] When he attempted to ask his mother to appeal to the appropriate authorities for redress of this grievance, as is his right under the law,[59] he was severely punished.[60]

Conclusion

We appeal to the Procurator General to prevent any recurrence of these arbitrary and illegal deprivations and punishments discussed in this memorandum. We also request that he investigate these incidents to determine if a pattern of discriminatory behavior exists, and to take necessary corrective action.

N O T E S

Some of the footnotes refer to affidavits not printed in this book, for purposes of brevity.

1. Statute on Procuracy, Supervision in the U.S.S.R. (hereinafter "Statute on the Procuracy"), Articles 32–37.

2. "Basic Principles of Legislation Pertaining to Correctional Labor of the USSR and the Union Republics" (hereinafter "Principles"), §1.
3. Commentary to §27 of Principles.
4. Principles, §36.
5. Feiga Shkolnik Affidavit.
6. Sonia Druk Affidavit; Eva Lisitzin Affidavit.
7. *Ibid.*
8. Musia Yagman Affidavit.
9. Henrietta Kissina Affidavit.
10. See also Boguslavsky Affidavit.
11. E.g., Shimon Levit Affidavit.
12. Article 37 of the Corrective Labor Code of the R.S.F.S.R. (hereinafter "Labor Code") provides that economic activity must be subordinate to reform and re-education of convicts.
13. Labor Code, Article 38.
14. Sonia Druk Affidavit; Eva Lisitzin Affidavit.
15. *Ibid.*
16. Boguslavsky Affidavit; Eva Butman Affidavit; Valery Vudka Affidavit.
17. *Ibid.*
18. Principles, §1.
19. Article123.
20. Constitution of the R.S.F.S.R., Article 127.
21. §5.
22. Affidavits of Yulia Dymshitz; Shimon Levit; Berta Chernoglaz; Valery Vudka; Chaim Grilius.
23. Affidavit of Berta Chernoglaz.
24. Affidavits of Sonia Druk; Eva Lisitzin.
25. Affidavit of Berta Chernoglaz.
26. Affidavit of Shimon Levit.
27. Affidavit of Chaim Grilius.
28. Affidavit of Valery Vudka.
29. Note Article 28 of United Nations Standard Minimum Rules for the Treatment of Prisoners.
30. General regime—Labor Code, Article 62; intensified regime Labor Code, Article 63; strict regime—Labor Code, Article 64; special regime—Labor Code, Article 65.
31. Labor Code, Article 30. See also Principles, Article 26.
32. Labor Code, Article 22.
33. Labor Code, Article 30.
34. Labor Code, Articles 28, 62–65.
35. Labor Code, Articles 53, 54.
36. *Ibid.*
37. Affidavit of Valery Vudka.
38. Article 124.
39. E.g., Constitution of the R.S.F.S.R., Article 128.
40. Criminal Code, Article 143.
41. The Labor Code obligates authorities to make known restrictive regulations to all inmates.
42. Affidavits of Sonia Druk; Eva Lisitzin.
43. *Ibid.*

44. Article 38.
45. Affidavit of Aaron Grilius.
46. Affidavit of Valery Vudka.
47. Affidavits of Aaron Grilius; Valery Vudka; Sonia Druk.
48. Principles, Article 1.
49. Labor Code, Article 43.
50. Commentary to Principles, Section 19.
51. Affidavits of Sonia Druk; Eva Lisitzin.
52. Affidavit of Eva Butman.
53. Affidavits of Pinchos Knokh; Meri Knokh; Musia Yagman; Henrietta Kissina.
54. Affidavit of Yulia Dymshitz.
55. Affidavits of Musia Yagman; Chaim Grilius.
56. Affidavit of Chaim Grilius.
57. Affidavit of Musia Yagman.
58. Affidavit of Mira Azernikov.
59. Labor Code, Article 36.
60. Affidavit of Mira Azernikov.

LEGAL MEMORANDUM IV

Legal Issues Relating to the Leningrad Trials

This memorandum develops several legal arguments raised in the petitions for Dymshitz, Kuznetsov, Knokh, S. Zalmanson, I. Zalmanson, V. Zalmanson, Fedorov, Murzhenko, and Mendelevich (Leningrad trial of December 24, 1970) and in those for Butman and M. Korenblit (Leningrad trial of May 20, 1971). The arguments contained in this memorandum all deal with alleged violations of Articles 15, 17, 64 and 93–1 of the Criminal Code of the R.S.F.S.R. (CC RSFSR), growing out of the alleged plan to hijack a Soviet airplane on June 15, 1970, in order to leave the Soviet Union.

I. Petitioners' Acts Did Not Constitute a Violation of Article 64(a)

Convicted prisoners Dymshitz, Kuznetsov, Mendelevich, Knokh, S. Zalmanson, V. Zalmanson, I. Zalmanson, Fedorov, Murzhenko, Butman, and M. Korenblit were convicted of preparation or attempt (Article 15) or complicity (Article 17) to commit treason (Article 64(a)), by participating in an alleged plan to leave the Soviet Union.

Petitioners respectfully submit that Article 64(a) is not, and was never intended to be, applicable to the conduct in which the defendants allegedly engaged. Their alleged conduct constituted a violation of Article 83, which prohibits "exit abroad . . . without the requisite passport or the permission of the proper authorities. . . ." Mendel Abramovich Bodnia, a co-defendant with all defendants listed above except Butman and M. Korenblit, was convicted under Article 83, not Article 64.

Article 64(a) defines treason as: "an act intentionally committed by a citizen of the U.S.S.R. to the detriment of the state independence, the territorial inviolability, or the military might of the U.S.S.R. . . ." It is clear from this definition that a defendant who violates this article must cause (or intend) certain results of his actions: *i.e.,* consequences which seriously affect important interests of the U.S.S.R.—its independence, its territorial inviolability, or its military might. A person who acts in such a way as, for example, to embarrass the U.S.S.R. or harm its prestige would not be guilty of treason unless his actions also worked to the detriment of one of those three important interests.

This interpretation of Article 64(a) is supported by the enumeration of six types of action which the statute specifies as categories—apparently exhaustive categories—of treasonous acts:

1. going over to the side of the enemy;
2. espionage;
3. transmission of a state or military secret to a foreign state;
4. flight abroad or refusal to return from abroad to the U.S.S.R.;
5. rendering aid to a foreign state in carrying on hostile activity against the U.S.S.R.; or
6. a conspiracy for the purpose of seizing power.

Five of the six categories clearly cover actions posing immediate and concrete danger to the security of the Soviet state. Universally accepted principles of statutory construction require that the sixth category—flight abroad or refusal to return—be construed in a manner consistent with the dominant purpose of the statute as evidenced by the other categories. This conclusion is further compelled by the definition of treason continued in the statute, as discussed above. Thus, even if a person's flight from the U.S.S.R. were to embarrass the state, it could not be considered treason unless it also endangered the state's independence, territorial inviolability, or military might.

It is clear that the act of leaving the U.S.S.R. without permission, when committed by a Soviet citizen, may constitute the *actus reus* that is required for a violation, either of Article 64(a) or Article 83. But it is also clear that this act alone, while sufficient to constitute a violation of Article 83, is not sufficient to constitute a violation of the far more serious Article 64(a).[1] For an illegal flight abroad to constitute treason under 64(a), the prosecution must establish that the act of illegal flight was "intentionally committed . . . to the detriment of the state independence, the territorial inviolability, or the military might of the U.S.S.R."[2] This additional element—which converts a relatively minor crime carrying a prison term of one to three years into a capital crime—must be fully proved at trial and may not be presumed.[3]

The standard applicable in determining guilt under Article 64(a) cannot be ignored when a person is prosecuted not for commission of the completed offense under 64(a) but only for preparation or attempt (Article 15) or complicity (Article 17) to violate Article 64(a).

To be sure, it is not necessary to prove under Article 64(a) that actual harm has occurred to the independence, territorial inviolability, or military might of the Soviet Union; it is enough to prove that such harm was intended.[4] But an intent to commit sufficiently serious anti-Soviet acts abroad is essential; it is certainly not enough that the act of leaving the country was motivated by anti-Soviet feelings. *

Several Soviet legal writings have argued that anti-Soviet motives convert an illegal exit into treason under 64(a). They distinguish between personal motives for the exit (which would constitute a violation of Article 83) and anti-Soviet motives (which would constitute a violation of Article 64(a).[5] It is respectfully submitted that this distinction is erroneous, and undercuts the purposes of Article 64(a). It ignores the definition of treason contained in the statute itself, a definition which requires certain specified intention before an action may be classified as treasonous.[6] A person leaving the Soviet Union out of anti-Soviet feelings may have no intention to engage in anti-Soviet activity once he has arrived at his point of destination. In this case, there would surely be no danger to the value protected by 64(a)—the external security of the state. On the other hand, a person leaving for personal reasons (such as economic or family reasons) may nonetheless have an intention to engage in serious anti-Soviet activities once he arrives at his point of destination; he may, for example, act out of mercenary impulses rather than for political reasons. A construction of the statute, under which the former but not the latter would be punished for treason, would be inconsistent with the fundamental purpose of the treason statute— to protect the external security of the U.S.S.R. Several Soviet authorities have commented on the inconsistency between such an approach and the underlying purpose of the statute. For this reason, several distinguished commentators hold that a conviction under Article 64(a) requires proof that the persons leaving the country

---

* The distinction between motive and intent is recognized by all legal systems. Motive is generally past-looking: it explains why an act was (or is being) engaged in. Intent is generally future-looking: it indicates a planned course of action. This distinction explains why criminal codes generally do not punish motive but often punish intent, at least when accompanied by certain kinds of prescribed conduct.

planned specific conduct abroad which would be harmful to the external security of the U.S.S.R. It is not enough that their departure may have been motivated by anti-Soviet feelings, or even that their past conduct was of an anti-Soviet character. This view has been recently expressed in a highly authoritative textbook published by the University of Moscow under the editorship of three leading Soviet criminal law scholars, Professors V. D. Menshagin, N. D. Durmanov, and G. A. Krigier.

The relevant passage reads as follows:

"An illegal crossing of the state border of the U.S.S.R. may be deemed treason only in a case where a citizen of the U.S.S.R. committed this act with an anti-Soviet purpose, *i.e.,* had an intention, having gone abroad, to engage in an activity detrimental to the state independence, territorial inviolability, or the military might of the U.S.S.R.: to transmit a state or a military secret to a foreign state, to participate in the anti-Soviet organizations, to publish in newspapers or to broadcast slanders against the Soviet state and social system, to be hired by a foreign intelligence," etc.[7]

Such treasonous design, it is correctly indicated by the same textbook (p. 36), must be proved and may never be presumed. In particular, it may not be inferred from the mere fact of an illegal flight abroad, even when it is proved also that the flight was motivated by anti-Soviet feelings.

The Supreme Court, in reviewing the cases of the defendants convicted of attempt or preparation to violate Article 64(a), referred to only one action possibly contemplated by some (not all) of those defendants on their arrival abroad: an intention to request political amnesty, presumably from Sweden, the intended destination. The language of the statute strongly suggests the type of anti-Soviet activity that a person must contemplate in order to violate Article 64(a). The activity must be of a type similar to espionage, transmission of state or military secrets, rendering aid to a hostile power, or conspiracy to seize power. It must, in other words, be directed against the external security of the U.S.S.R.

It is respectfully submitted that the act of requesting political asylum is not an anti-Soviet act of that character. Seeking political asylum does not even remotely resemble those actions which Soviet law explicitly identifies as to the external security of the state, *i.e.,* actions exhaustively listed in Articles 64–65, CC RSFSR.

Moreover, the U.S.S.R. Constitution provides in Article 129 for "the right to asylum for foreign citizens."[8] The Soviet government has always declared its respect for the independence and sovereignty of foreign states and its fidelity to the principle of noninterference in their internal affairs. Thus, providing political asylum to a foreign citizen cannot be viewed as detrimental to the foreign state's security. Similarly, the action of some of the defendants in seeking political asylum from a friendly country—such as Sweden—cannot, in itself, be regarded under Soviet law as detrimental to the external security of the U.S.S.R.

II. *Incorrect Application of Article 93–1, CC RSFSR*

It is respectfully submitted that application of Article 93–1, CC RSFSR, to these cases constitutes a substantial violation of law.

In order to constitute "stealing [*khishchenie*] of state or social property on an especially large scale," an act must of course correspond with the legal concept of "stealing."

The courts in these cases virtually ignored this legal requirement.

Judicial decisions of the Soviet high courts as well as Soviet legal literature on the subject matter have long been unanimous in their views that the legal concept of "stealing" involves more than mere physical taking of property away from the owner's control. It has unanimously been held that stealing involves taking of property with intent to keep it or otherwise to deal with it as with one's own, and hence with intent to deprive the owner of his property *permanently*.

This basic position of the Soviet criminal law has been strongly emphasized by the Decree of the Plenum of the Supreme Court of the U.S.S.R. of March 31, 1962—confirmed by the later decisions of the same court.[9]

This interpretation has been supported and further developed by Soviet legal scholars. Academician A. A. Piontkovskil in his fundamental work gives the following definition: ". . . stealing of state or social property is an intentional converting, by anybody, of state property, collective-farm property, or other public property into one's own."[10] On the next page he makes it clear that by "converting" he means disposition in fact, not a transfer in law. Addressing himself to the question of a requisite intent, Professor Piontkovskil continues: "The Supreme Court of the U.S.S.R. in the decrees of its Plenum and through its judicial panels has repeatedly drawn to the attention of the courts that it is necessary to establish the actor's intention to convert the state or public property into his own. . . ."[11] ". . . Thus, from the subjective point of view having appropriation as the purpose is characteristic of every kind of stealing."[12] This obviously includes the stealing covered by Article 93–1. Academician Piontkovskil's conclusion that an act of stealing requires an intention permanently to appropriate the property is unanimously shared by the Soviet criminal law writers.[13]

The only possible conclusion that can be drawn from the general concept of "stealing," outlined above, is that an act committed without the intention of appropriating state or public property may not constitute the crime of stealing. This is especially true in cases of unlawful temporary use of means of transportation, since the Soviet law treats this kind of act as a separate, specifically defined crime (see Article 212, CC RSFSR).

"Temporary use of the state or public property, without a purpose to appropriate it, may not be deemed stealing. . . . To drive away a vehicle of transport without the purpose of appropriating it, but with the purpose of taking a ride, and then abandoning it, may not be deemed stealing."[14]

Since the courts, in the cases here considered, virtually ignored the fundamental legal principle that the defendants could be guilty of stealing only if they intended permanently to appropriate state property, the judgments neither articulate factual findings on this issue nor explain the legal theory of the decision. This, in itself, is in violation of Articles 301, 303, and 314, CCP RSFSR. A decision that lacks any evidentiary basis and is based on assumptions is in violation of Articles 301 and 309, CCP. A decision made tacitly, *i.e.,* without articulation of the grounds in the judgment, deprives the defendants of a fair opportunity to challenge it in cassational and supervisory proceedings in violation of Articles 301 and 314, CCP. Moreover, a conclusion that defendants had intended to appropriate the plane permanently would be contrary to the factual circumstances of the case.

1. it is a matter of common knowledge and well-established international practice that hijacked aircraft are promptly returned to their owners as a matter of course;

2. permanent appropriation of the plane under the circumstances was a sheer impossibility; and it was an impossibility known to the petitioners at all times before their arrest;

3. the prosecution's own theory was based on the assumption that the defendants were motivated by political not mercenary considerations.

It follows that the application of Article 93–1, CC, in the present case was an error.

It may be added that the Soviet legislature apparently felt that the criminal law prevailing in the U.S.S.R. prior to January 1973 was not providing adequate protection against hijacking. The new law enacted by the Presidium of the Supreme Soviet of the U.S.S.R. on January 3, 1973, remedied the gap.[15]

III. *Excessive Severity of the Sentences*

1. Even if Articles 64(a) and 93–1, CC RSFSR, were deemed applicable to defendants' conduct, the penalties imposed on them are excessive according to the standards of sentencing under Soviet law.

2. A well-established general rule is that so-called uncompleted crimes, *i.e.*, preparation and attempt, should not be punished as severely as their completed counterparts, since they represent a lower degree of social danger.[16] It has even been suggested by Professor Duramanov that special sanctions should be established for preparation and attempt, with the statutory minimum fixed at one-half the punishment for completed crimes.[17]

Furthermore, under Soviet law there is a well-recognized distinction between an *attempt* to commit a crime and a mere *preparation* to commit a crime. The borderline between those two early stages of criminal action has been characterized by Academician A. A. Piontkovskil as follows:

"Attempt creates immediate danger of the criminal harm, whereas preparation means creation of conditions for the future criminal actions."

". . . attempt . . . already in itself contains a real possibility of the criminal result (harm); attempt is a beginning of perpetration containing immediate danger for the value protected by the criminal law."[18]

The textbook cited in footnote 7, supra, discusses the distinction between preparation and attempt in the context of Article 63(a):

"If a citizen of the U.S.S.R. until the moment of his arrest . . . did not directly start crossing the border, his action should be deemed a preparation to treason" ("neprosredstrvenno k perekhodu granitsy eshche ne pristupil"), p. 35.

The defendants here were arrested at a much earlier stage: the first group was arrested at the airport, before even boarding the plane, and the second group was arrested far away from the airport in the forest. Thus, even if successful completion of their plans could properly be deemed to have resulted in a violation of Article 64(a), they should have been convicted of preparation to commit such a crime, rather than of an attempt to commit the crime.

This error in legal classification of the defendants' actions may have detrimentally affected the courts' decisions on the sentences.

A recent commentary to CC RSFSR suggests that "For attempt, and even more particularly for preparation, a punishment equal to the statutory maximum may not, as a rule, be imposed."[19]

3. While sentencing for uncompleted crimes the court shall take into account "the degree to which the criminal intention is carried out" (Article 15, paragraph 4, CC RSFSR).

This provision brings to the sentencing process another rule, consistent with the one mentioned in paragraph 2: the more remote the completion of the crime, the more lenient should be the sentence. Hence, preparation, other circumstances being equal, is entitled to more lenient treatment than attempt: more advanced (so-called completed) attempts should be treated more severely than less advanced ones (incompleted attempts).[20]

4. Sentencing practices of the Soviet courts seem to be consistent with these general guidelines.

"The kind of attempt"—reports a recent criminal textbook[21]—"is taken into account by the courts in the sentencing. *In 36% of the cases of uncompleted attempts, sentences were equal to the statutory minimum, or Article 43, CC, has been applied, i.e., sentences below the statutory minimum have been imposed.*

"*. . . Preparation in general is punished even more leniently.*"[22] (Emphasis added.)

Other highly authoritative sources report that in practice criminal liability for preparation is rarely imposed: instead, charges are dropped, because of the insignificant degree of social danger of preparatory acts.[23]

It has been suggested in the commentary published by the Procuracy of the U.S.S.R. that charges for preparation should be dropped even in such serious cases as, for example, arson (punishable by up to ten years deprivation of freedom).[24]

5. It is further respectfully submitted that the Supreme Court of the U.S.S.R. in its own sentencing practice has found the uncompleted character of an otherwise serious crime (attempted rape of a minor) to be a ground for reducing the sentence below the statutory minimum. This has been done in supervisory proceedings initiated by the protest of the Deputy President of the U.S.S.R. Supreme Court.[25]

6. In the case of A. Meredov referred to above,[26] the Supreme Court of the U.S.S.R. reduced the sentence to *a half of the statutory minimum* for an attempted rape of a minor on the grounds of the following mitigating circumstances:

"Meredov has no criminal record. He has a family. The case shows no harmful consequences for a victim."[27] It is submitted that all of the grounds relied upon by the Supreme Court of the U.S.S.R. in the case of Meredov would be applicable to most of defendants in these cases. The central point—that there were no harmful consequences—is applicable here to all the defendants. . . .

9. In the light of the above, it seems that the sentences are highly excessive and were imposed in disregard of the rules, standards, and practices prevailing under the Soviet law.

It is respectfully submitted that the said rules, standards, and practices require substantial reduction of the sentences pursuant to Article 43, CC RSFSR.

June 10, 1974   /s/ TELFORD TAYLOR

NOTES

1. G. Z. Anashkin, *Otvetstvennost' za izmenu rodine i shpionazh* (Moscow, 1964), p. 105; V. I. Kurlianskii and M. P. Mikhajlov, eds., *Osobo opasnye gosudarstvennye prestupleniia* (Moscow, 1963), p. 86; M. I. Iakubovich and A. Vladimirov, eds., *Gosudarstvennye prestupleniia* (Moscow, 1961), p. 27; *Kurs sovetskogo ugolovnogo prava. V shesti tomakh. Chast' osobennaia.* Tom IV (Moscow, 1970, pp. 90–91; *Kurs sovetskogo ugolovnogo prava. Chast' osobennaia.* Tom 3 (Leningrad, 1973), p. 136.
2. Anashkin, note 1, pp. 156–157; Kurlianskii, Mikhajlov, note 1, *Kommentarii k ugolovnomu kodeksu RSFSR* (Moscow, 1971), p. 158; *Kurs* 1970, note 1, Tom IV, p. 85; *Kurs* 1973, note 1, Tom 3, pp. 118, 136.
3. *Teoriia dokazatelstv v sovetskom ugolovnom protsesse. Chast' obschchaia* (Moscow, 1966), pp. 200–201.
4. Kurlianskii, Mikhajlov, note 1, pp. 77–78; *Prokuratura Soiuza SSSR, Nauchno-prakticheskii kommentarii ugolovnogo kodeksa RSFSR (Izdaniie vtoroe)* (Moscow, 1964), p. 154.
5. See Anashkin, p. 105; Kurlianskii *et al.*, pp. 85–86; Iakubovich *et al.*, p. 27. The sources cited here seem not to distinguish between anti-Soviet motives and anti-Soviet purposes. Compare also *Kurs* 1970, Tom IV, pp. 90–91; *Kurs* 1973, Tom 3, pp. 136–138.
6. *Kurs* 1973, Tom 3, p. 137.
7. V. D. Menshagin, N. D. Durmanov, G. A. Krigier, *Sovetskoe ugolovnoe pravo. Osobennaia chast'. Izdatelstvo Moskovskogo Universiteta,* 1971, p. 35.
8. See also Article 83, §2, CC RSFSR.
9. *Bull.,* U.S.S.R. Supreme Court, 1962, No. 3, pp. 26–34, especially see paragraphs 7, 8, and 12. See also later decisions of the same court: Case of Dabyshev, Ruling of the Military Division of August 31, 1967; Case of Draganov, Ruling of the Criminal Division of February 15, 1971. *Sbornik postanovlenii Plenuma i opredelenii kolegii Verkhovnogo Suda SSR po ugolovnym delam* (Moscow, 1973), pp. 169, 184 resp.
10. *Kurs sovetskogo ugolovnogo prava. V shesti tomakh. Chast' osobennaia.* Tom IV (Moscow, 1970), p. 307.
11. *Ibid.,* p. 308.
12. *Ibid.,* pp. 325, 327.
13. Compare: *Sovetskoe ugolovnoe pravo. Osobennaia chast'. Izdatelstvo Moskovskogo Universiteta,* 1971, p. 107; *Kurs sovetskogo ugolovnogo prava. Chast' osobennaia.* Tom 3. *Izdatelstvo Leningratskogo Universiteta,* 1973, p. 350; *Kommentarii k ugolovnomu kodeksu RSFSR* (Moscow, 1971), p. 193; *Ugolovnoe pravo. Chast' osobennaia* (Moscow, 1969), p. 96; *Ugolovnoe pravo. Chast' osobennaia* (Moscow, 1968), p. 121.
14. *Kurs sovetskogo ugolovnogo prava,* Tom IV, *supra,* note 10, p. 327; U.S.S.R. Supreme Court Ruling in the Case of Dabyshev, *supra,* note 9, at pp. 184, 185: *Obvineniie v Khishchenii litsa, samovolno ugnavshego mashinu, mozhet byt' priznano pravilnym lish pri dokazannosti umysla na prisvoeniie mashiny.*

15. *Ukaz Prezidiuma Verkhovnogo Soveta SSSR* of January 3, 1973. *Vedomosti Verkhovnogo Soveta SSSR,* 1973, No. 1, Item 3.
16. *Sovetskoe ugolovnoe pravo. Chast' obshchaia. Izdatelstvo Moskovskogo Universiteta,* 1969, p. 223; *Kurs sovetskogo ugolovnogo prava. V shesti tomakh.* Tom II (Moscow, 1970), p. 408; *Kommentarii k ugolovnomu kodeksu RSFSR* (Moscow, 1971), p. 43; *Prokuratura Soiuza SSSR Nauchno-prakticheskii kommentarii ugolovnogo kodeksa RSFSR (Izd. vtoroe)* (Moscow, 1964), p. 41; N. D. Durmanov, *Stadii soversheniia prestupleniia po sovetskomu ugolovnomu pravu* (Moscow, 1955), pp. 185–186; F. G. Burchak, *Uchenie o souchastii po sovetskomu ugolovnomu pravu* (Kiev, 1969), pp. 192–193.
17. Durmanov, note 16, p. 186.
18. *Kurs sovetskogo ugolovnogo prava. V shesti tomakho.* Tom II (Moscow, 1970), p. 409.
19. *Kommentarii* (1971), p. 43.
20. See authorities cited in note 16.
21. *Sovetskoe ugolovnoe pravo. Chast' obshchaia* (Moscow, 1972).
22. *Ibid.,* p. 254.
23. *Nauchno-prakticheskii kommentarii,* note 16, p. 41; *Kurs sovetskogo ugolovnogo prava,* note 16, Tom II (Moscow, 1970), p. 408.
24. *Nauchno-prakticheskii kommentarii,* note 16, p. 41.
25. Ruling of the Criminal Division of the U.S.S.R. Supreme Court of August 15, 1969, Case of Meredov. *Bull.,* U.S.S.R. Supreme Court (1969), No. 5, pp. 30–31.
26. *Supra,* note 25.
27. *Ibid.*

D. Affidavits

1. My name is Pinchos Knokh. I am a former citizen of the U.S.S.R., where I resided at Daugavpils, Latvian S.S.R. Since April 14, 1971, I have been a citizen of Israel and I reside at Kibbuts Reshafim.

2. I am the brother of Leib (Arie) Knokh, who is now confined at Perm Camp, which is located in the Permsky region, based on the judgment of the Leningrad City Court on December 24, 1970, sentencing him to ten years of confinement.

3. I attended the trial of my brother at the Leningrad City Court between December 15, 1970, and December 24, 1970, and I recall the proceedings in detail.

4. I witnessed the interruption of the testimony offered by Lev Korenblit and his forcible eviction from the courtroom. At the time immediately preceding the interruption of his testimony, Korenblit was offering evidence bearing on the defense of my brother as well as the other defendants at the trial. In particular, he was testifying about the events that occurred at the home of Mark Dymshitz on the evening of June 13, 1970, shortly before the arrest of my brother and of the other defendants on the morning of June 15, 1970. On the basis of my observation, the interruption of Korenblit's testimony occurred at the time that Korenblit began to discuss the attitudes of Dymshitz toward leaving the Soviet Union. Korenblit was obviously prevented from completing his testimony on matters clearly relevant to the charge against the defendants.

5. Based on my observation at the trial, the Procurator confirmed, in his behavior and offers of proof, an obligation on the part of the prosecution to prove an intent to injure the Soviet Union after crossing the border into Sweden. On this issue of intent to harm the Soviet Union, the Procurator presented to the court the following:

   1. allegation of a plan to hold a press conference in Sweden;
   2. an "Appeal," written before the events in question; and
   3. items of literature which the Procurator described as anti-Soviet.

6. Regarding the issue of whether or not the literature introduced at the trial was in fact anti-Soviet in nature, there was no testimony, expert or otherwise, nor references by the Procurator or the Judge to any prior determination, nor references contained in any protocols, concerning the nature of the content of the materials. On the basis of my observation, the Judge recognized and acknowledged at the trial that the issue of whether or not the literature was anti-Soviet was a relevant legal issue. I know this because the Judge permitted the defendants to argue whether the literature was anti-Soviet or not. I heard some of the defendants engage in disputation with the Judge about whether or not the literature was anti-Soviet. On the basis of my observations of the trial, the Procurator made no effort whatsoever to refute the claims of my brother and other defendants that the literature was not anti-Soviet.

7. With regard to certain other issues at the trial, the Judge publicly read the protocols prepared by expert witnesses. One of these issues was whether the gun carried by one of the defendants was in fact an operative weapon. Another issue on which expert testimony was introduced was the mental condition of some of the defendants.

AFFIDAVIT OF POLINA KORENBLIT

1. My name is Polina Korenblit. I am a former citizen of the U.S.S.R. and a resident of Leningrad. I have been a citizen of Israel since April 17, 1972, and I reside at Haifa, Bodengeimer 88-12.

2. I am the wife of Mikhail Korenblit, who is now confined at camp 17 Mordovia, based on the judgment of the Leningrad City Court in May 1971, sentencing him to seven years of confinement.

3. My husband testified as a witness at the previous trial held at the Leningrad City Court from December 15 to December 24, 1970.

4. Based on conversations that I have had with my husband while visiting him in the prison camp in 1971 and 1972, I have learned about his appearance as a witness at the December 1970 Leningrad trial. My husband was forcibly evicted from the courtroom while testifying at that trial. At the time immediately preceding the interruption of his testimony, my husband was testifying about the events that occurred at the home of Mark Dymshitz on the evening of June 13, shortly before the arrest of the defendants on the morning of June 15, 1970. In particular he had just commenced testifying about a conversation which he had had with Dymshitz on that occasion. I have learned from my husband that my husband intended to testify to the fact that he had discussed with Dymshitz

infiltration into the group by agents of the KGB in order to stimulate the crime. According to my husband, the interruption of his testimony prevented him from being able to testify regarding this conversation. In any event, whatever testimony my husband would have given, he was deprived of the right to complete the testimony which he was offering on behalf of the defendants on trial.

Affidavit of Eva Butman

1. My name is Eva Butman. I am a former citizen of the U.S.S.R. and a resident of Leningrad. I emigrated to Israel on July 12, 1973, where I am now a resident of Jerusalem.

2. I am the wife of Hillel Butman, who is confined at Camp 35, Perm, based on the judgment of the Leningrad City Court in May 1971, sentencing him to ten years confinement.

3. Prior to my husband's trial, my husband made it clear to the authorities that he desired to defend himself and did not want a lawyer assigned to his case. My husband had completed legal training at the Law Institute, from which he received a diploma in 1954. Therefore, he was fully authorized to work as a jurist, and he had also worked as an investigator for the police for several years. When a lawyer from Moscow went to visit my husband, he refused to see him on the grounds that he intended to defend himself. I was informed by the investigator in charge of my husband's case that my husband had no right to defend himself. Despite my husband's objections, a lawyer, chosen by the Leningrad Collegium, was appointed to his case, and my husband was informed that he had no right to refuse this lawyer.

Affidavit of Sima Kaminsky

My name is Sima Kaminsky, and I am the wife of Lassal Kaminsky, who is currently serving a five-year sentence as a result of a conviction before a Leningrad court in May 1971. I am currently a citizen of Israel, living in Jerusalem. Before my emigration to Israel in October 1971, I was a citizen of the Soviet Union residing at Leningrad.

1. After my husband's arrest on June 15, 1970, I set out to find him a lawyer. I decided upon an advocate named Rozhdestvensky to represent my husband. I purposely selected a non-Jewish lawyer because we believed that a good non-Jewish lawyer would be able to defend my husband more vigorously and with less fear of pressure from the authorities than a Jewish lawyer. I knew that Rozhdestvensky had the necessary permit (*dopusk*) allowing him to represent defendants in political trials.

2. After the trial, I learned that advocate Rozhdestvensky had lost his right to practice law. I learned that the incident which led to his losing his right had occurred before the trial, during the investigation of my husband. I also learned that before the trial, Rozhdestvensky had been told that he had been caught engaging in an improper act and that he would be dealt with after the completion of the trial. He was told that he could, however, complete my husband's trial.

3. Advocate Rozhdestvensky advised my husband to admit partial guilt, even though I objected and though my husband did not want to admit any guilt whatsoever. However, my husband was forced by circumstances to rely on Rozhdestvensky's advice.

4. I know that my husband was not aware, before or during the trial, that Rozhdestvensky had been told that his future as a lawyer would be decided after the trial. I also was not aware of this until after the trial.

5. Had my husband and I known of the situation confronting him, we would certainly have insisted on his removal from the case and on the appointment of a new lawyer who was not facing the loss of his right to practice law.

6. We deliberately selected Rozhdestvensky because we felt it necessary to have a lawyer who would not be fearful of the consequences of representing my husband. It is obvious that a lawyer who knows that immediately after the trial he is going to confront a serious accusation that might result in the loss of his right to practice law will not feel entirely free to challenge the authorities in the way a good advocate must be prepared to do when the occasion calls for it. Moreover, an advocate facing such a serious prospect cannot possibly devote his full energies and attention to the defense of another person when he himself is preoccupied with a threat to his entire career.

7. It is my sincere view that my husband's right to effective representation, guaranteed by the law, was violated by the fact that his defense was conducted by an advocate who was facing the loss of his power to practice law at the time of the trial and neither the authorities nor his advocate advised him or his family of this situation.

AFFIDAVIT OF SHIMON LEVIT

I, Shimon Levit, now a citizen of the State of Israel, residing at Bnei-Brak, do hereby depose and state:

1. I was born in Kishinev, U.S.S.R., in 1947, and remained a citizen of the Soviet Union until 1973, when I emigrated to Israel, where I arrived on the first of February, 1973.

2. On June 30, 1971, I was convicted under Articles 67 and 69 of the Moldavian Criminal Code by the Supreme Court of Moldavia, and sentenced to imprisonment for two years.

3. After my arrest and during my interrogation, I was not permitted any communication with my parents or other relatives or friends, or allowed any legal counsel. After the interrogation was completed, I was allowed to see the accusation against me and the supporting dossier. In the dossier was a memorandum by *Glavlit,* which classified the various documents which had been seized during the search of my home and the homes of the others accused, who were eventually tried with me before the Supreme Court of Moldavia.

4. These classifications were: anti-Soviet, Zionist, nationalistic, dangerous, not for wide use, and defective. Only literature classified as anti-Soviet can be the basis for criminal charges under Moldavian Articles 67 and 69. In the *Glavlit* memorandum only a few of the documents which had been seized from our home were described as anti-Soviet, while a large number of others were classified as Zionist or nationalistic.

5. During the trial, the presiding judge of the court announced that the court was not bound by the classifications of the literature upon which the prosecution relied. In its verdict, the court treated as anti-Soviet a number of documents which were not so classified in the memorandum. The judge did not call any experts and did not give any reason for determining those other documents to be anti-Soviet.

6. At the trial, only about half of the witnesses who had testified during the investigation, and whose testimony was relied on by the prosecution, were called to testify before the court. For example, Latzman did not appear in Court, and Shpilberg, although he was brought to Kishinev, did not testify in Court.

7. Under the Code of Criminal Procedure of the Moldavian Republic, a convicted prisoner is entitled to take a copy of his accusation and of the verdict with him to his place of confinement. I was not permitted to do this. While in camp I wrote letters to the Moldavian authorities requesting that I be sent copies of these documents. Finally I received a reply that I could examine the documents at an office in a remote city.

8. After my conviction I was sent to Camp No. 3 near Potma in Mordovia and remained there throughout the term of my imprisonment. Together with me at Camp No. 3 were Israel and Vulf Zalmanson from the first trial of Jews in Leningrad, Oleg Frolov from the trial in Ryazan, Mogilever and Dreizner from the second Leningrad trial, and Chernoglaz from the Kishinev trial in which I was also convicted.

9. In Camp No. 3 there were about 450 prisoners. These included eight Jews, and small groups of "Nationalists" (a group which included the Jews, Ukrainians, Lithuanians, etc.), so-called "democratic" dissenters, so-called "Russian Nationalists" (which included monarchists), and a religious group, which included Baptists and Jehovah's Witnesses. All these groups together made up about a quarter of the entire group of prisoners.

10. The other persons, comprising about three-quarters of the total, had all been convicted of crimes committed as collaborators when the German Nazi forces invaded the Soviet Union during World War II. Between that war and my time in Camp No. 3, there had been two amnesties pursuant to which many former Nazi collaborators were released. Those who were still in jail while I was in the camp were serving long sentences imposed because their crimes had included one or more murders.

11. The Nazi collaborators were given for their work the easier and better jobs, in which the fulfillment of the work quotas was possible. The Jewish prisoners were given the hardest and most unpleasant work, for which the quotas were filled at an impossibly high level. For example, the Jewish prisoner Vulf Zalmanson, who was an engineer, was at first given technical work in the automobile wheel factory in which most of the prisoners worked. But a few weeks after his arrival, when the camp authorities learned that he was a Jew convicted at the so-called "Leningrad Hijacking" trial, they gave him hard and disagreeable physical labor, with the other Jews. Meanwhile, the Nazi collaborators were given jobs as clerks, security guards, etc., and some of them were referred to as "brigadiers." The result of these conditions was that the Jews were constantly in difficulty for not fulfilling the work quotas, and lost their privileges in connection with food parcels, visits, etc., while the Nazi collaborators got favored treatment.

AFFIDAVIT OF YAAKOV NISSAN

1. My name is Yaakov Nissan and I am a citizen of Israel. I was formerly a citizen of the U.S.S.R., residing in Derbent. I emigrated to Israel on October 28, 1974.

2. I am the brother of the wife of Pinkhas Pinkhasov, who is now confined at the correction-labor camp in the village of Bolshoy Nadim, Derbentsky Rayon, Kalmikskaya A.S.S.R., under the verdict of the City Court of Derbent entered on November 13, 1973, sentencing him to five years deprivation of freedom.

3. I was present in Derbent at the time that Pinkhasov was arrested, and I am personally familiar with the attempts of his family

members to obtain a defense lawyer for him. Pinkhasov's family wanted him to be represented by advocate Wexler from Moscow. But the Derbent authorities informed the family that Wexler would not be permitted to represent Pinkhasov and that only the local advocate Ovadya Ilyaev could be Pinkhasov's lawyer. Advocate Ilyaev was subjected to intimidation and threats by the authorities and therefore refused to submit the cassational appeal. For that reason, Pinkhasov submitted the appeal himself.

4. I attended Pinkhasov's entire trial on November 12 and 13, 1973, and personally observed the following.

5. Approximately eleven persons for whom Pinkhasov had done carpentry work were called as witnesses by the prosecution to testify against Pinkhasov. But not one witness substantiated the accusation that Pinkhasov had overcharged his customers. All testified that Pinkhasov had charged only the correct official price determined by his factory. They testified that any additional payments or gifts of food or drink made to Pinkhasov were owing to Pinkhasov for additional work which he performed (*e.g.,* for transportation of materials; for overtime and Sunday work; for use of his son as an assistant). No witness had a personal claim against Pinkhasov.

6. For the defense there were no witnesses called except Pinkhasov himself. He denied his guilt completely. When he attempted to state his belief that he was being prosecuted in retaliation for his plan to emigrate to Israel, the judge interrupted and forbade him to speak.

7. During a recess in the trial, one of the people's assessors, Riya Mishayeva, informed Pinkhasov's family that she had learned that the prosecution against Pinkhasov was a result of his application to emigrate. Mishayeva informed the family that, according to the judge, if Pinkhasov were to give up his desire to go to Israel and were to persuade his wife and children to return to the U.S.S.R., the prosecution would be dropped and Pinkhasov would be given a new apartment and a new job.

8. I have learned something of the condition of Pinkhasov's confinement through an uncle of mine who was previously in the same labor camp as Pinkhasov but was released in the fall of 1974. I saw my uncle in Derbent before my departure for Israel, and he reported that Pinkhasov, who is an amputee with one leg as a result of a work accident in 1959, fell and injured his hip in the camp.

9. My mother, with whom I emigrated to Israel on October 28, 1974, was warned by the KGB authorities, before our departure from the U.S.S.R., that if she spoke publicly and protested about Pinkhasov's case, Pinkhasov's conditions of confinement would be made worse.

Affidavit of Valery Vudka

I, Valery Vudka, now a citizen of the State of Israel, residing at Holon, Atarot 120/8, Kirvat-Sharet, do hereby depose and state that:

1. I was born in Pavlograd, U.S.S.R., in 1950, and was a citizen of the Soviet Union until February, 1973, when I emigrated to Israel.

2. I am the younger brother of Yuri Vudka, who was convicted under Articles 70 and 72 of the Criminal Code of the R.S.F.S.R. on February 19, 1970, by the District Court of Ryazan, and was sentenced to imprisonment for seven years.

3. I myself was convicted at the same trial and under the same articles, and was sentenced to imprisonment for three years, from August 1970 to August 1973. Two others convicted in the same trial and under the same articles—Shimon Grilius and Oleg Frolov, were each sentenced to imprisonment for five years.

4. After my conviction and the failure of my appeal, I was taken with my brother to Camp 19 near Potma in Mordavia. I remained in this camp from July 1970 to March 1971, when I was removed to the prison in Vladimir, and I remained in Vladimir until the end of my three-year term of imprisonment.

5. At about the time that I was transferred from the jail in Ryazan to Camp No. 19, my brother and I determined to observe the Jewish religious requirements with respect to the wearing of beards and yarmulkas, and eating only kosher food. At Camp No. 19 and subsequently in Vladimir, I refused to eat the prison meat because it was not kosher, and insisted on wearing a beard and a yarmulka. The camp authorities did not forcibly shave me or remove the yarmulke, but I suffered adverse discrimination and many penalties because of my insistence on these religious observances.

6. At Camp No. 19 the prisoners were allowed to purchase five rubles' worth of extra food each month. If the work quotas were fulfilled, the purchase of an additional two rubles was authorized, and if the quotas were exceeded, additional purchase allowances were supposed to be earned. The work assigned to me was cutting and carrying wood, which was very strenuous and difficult, but it was possible for me to fulfill the quota. However, I was not paid the two rubles which were due to me, because of discrimination against me for observance of the Jewish religious customs. I then abandoned my efforts to fulfill the quotas, and this resulted in penalties imposed by the camp commandant and eventually led to my transfer to Vladimir.

7. Among the other prisoners at Camp No. 19 were many who

had been convicted of crimes committed as collaborators with the German Nazi invaders during World War II. Some of them had been members of the Armed Forces led by General Vlasov, whose forces fought with the German Nazis against the Soviet forces. Among them was Staplinski, who had been an officer in the Vlasov forces. Another former Nazi collaborator was Balashov. These former Nazi collaborators worked in cooperation with the Soviet prison authorities and in consequence were given better jobs, in which fulfilling or exceeding the quotas was easily possible, and were also allowed additional privileges in receiving parcels from relatives and in purchasing food, including food illegally purchased from people who lived near the camp. Those former Nazi collaborators actively stirred up anti-Semitism among the other prisoners.

8. I was sent to Vladimir by order of a special tribunal which came to Camp No. 19. When I appeared before the tribunal, the camp commandant read to the members a list of the supposed offenses which I committed. The chairman of the tribunal ordered me to remove my yarmulka. After I had explained that my religion did not permit me to do this, the tribunal conferred briefly and then ordered me to Vladimir. My brother Yuri was sent to Vladimir in March 1973, under much the same circumstances. The tribunal before which I appeared never asked me for any explanation of the offenses of which the camp commandant had accused me.

9. The prison regime in Vladimir is very strict. During the first few months the food ration is wholly insufficient, consisting of only about 500 grams of bread and 60 grams of herring each day, with a little soup and porridge. No additional purchases are permitted. The prisoner is allowed outside the cell in the open air only one half-hour per day, and is given no work to do. He is permitted two short visits from relatives each year. He wears a special uniform. The electric light in his cell burns all day and at all times, and in the summer the cell is intolerably hot. I saw no former Nazi collaborators in Vladimir, and it was common knowledge that they were seldom sent there because they cooperate with the camp authorities.

10. I learned while in prison that Shimon Grilius and Josif Mendelevich also had serious trouble with the camp authorities because they insisted on growing beards, wearing yarmulkas, and rejecting non-kosher food.

AFFIDAVIT OF FEIGA SHKOLNIK

1. My name is Feiga Shkolnik. I am a former citizen of the U.S.S.R. and resident of Vinnitsa. I arrived in Israel on December 31, 1973, where I am now a resident of Beersheva.

2. I am the wife of Isaac Rafailovich Shkolnik who has been confined at Perm since August 1973, based on the judgment of the military tribunal of the Trans-Carpathian military district, Vinnitsa, on April 11, 1973, sentencing him to seven years confinement.

3. I retained the services of Advocate Makarenko to defend my husband at the trial. I was informed that Makarenko was the only lawyer available in Vinnitsa with the *dopusk* required by the KGB. I was dissatisfied with Makarenko's conduct of my husband's defense because from the very start he assumed my husband was guilty and made every effort to persuade my husband to plead guilty. He also refused to discuss fully my husband's case with me and offered me absolutely no information about the trial, answering only specific questions which I asked.

4. Shortly after my husband's conviction by the Military Tribunal, while visiting him in the Vinnitsa prison, I made an effort to communicate with my husband about Makarenko and the cassational appeal. The guard in attendance refused to permit me to speak to my husband about this subject.

5. After my husband's conviction, I requested Advocate Makarenko to file a cassational appeal. He originally declined to do so; therefore, I retained the services of another lawyer named Sarri, to whom I had been referred by the Moscow Collegium. Sarri immediately went to the headquarters of the Military Tribunal at Lvov, studied my husband's case, and received permission to visit him in the Vinnitsa prison. Sarri went to the prison on April 19, 1973, but despite the permission given him by the authorities at Lvov, the prison officials did not permit him to see my husband. While Sarri waited at the prison, Makarenko was called and came to the prison. Makarenko and the prison officials advised my husband that he should not see Sarri and required him to sign a written statement authorizing Makarenko as his lawyer. Consequently, Sarri was not able to meet my husband. Prior to his attempt to see my husband, Sarri had filed a written cassational appeal with the Military Tribunal at Lvov. After he was denied access to my husband, he filed a complaint with the authorities in Moscow concerning the obstruction of his attempt to act on my husband's behalf. I and my husband's parents filed similar complaints with the Supreme Court of the U.S.S.R., the Supreme Court of the Ukrainian Republic, and the Minister of Justice.

6. I never at any time retained the services of Makarenko to file a cassational appeal on my husband's behalf. After Sarri attempted to see my husband, however, Makarenko did file an appeal which he back-dated to April 16, the day before Sarri's visit. Several days before the cassational appeal, I went to the Moscow

Military Collegium of the Supreme Court and attempted to file a dismissal of Makarenko, but was not permitted to do so.

7. Based on these facts, it is clear that my husband was deprived of the counsel of his, and of his family's, choice, and that certain authorities conspired with Makarenko in depriving my husband of this choice.

AFFIDAVIT OF RIYA MISHAYEVA

1. My name is Riya Mishayeva and I am a citizen of Israel, residing at Shderot. I was formerly a citizen of the U.S.S.R., residing in Derbent. I emigrated to Israel on February 7, 1974.

2. Before I emigrated to Israel, I was a member of the Communist party for seven years, I was a member of the local Soviet in Derbent, and I had worked for eighteen years in a candy factory in Derbent.

3. In November 1973, I was serving my official turn as a People's Assessor for cases which came before the City Court of Derbent. I had been on the list of People's Assessors for five years and had judged many, many cases.

4. One of the cases on which I sat as a People's Assessor in November 1973 was the prosecution of Pinkhas Pinkhasov, who was a Jewish carpenter from Derbent. Pinkhasov was charged under the R.S.F.S.R. Criminal Code, Article 92 (misappropriation of state or public property committed through appropriation, embezzlement, or misuse of one's official position; punishable by deprivation of freedom up to four years) and Article 156 (deceiving of clients, cheating in measures and weights, raising of determined retail prices; punishable by deprivation of freedom up to two years). The judge was named Rasmasanov (of Lezginian origin) and there was a second People's Assessor.

5. I studied the file on Pinkhasov's case and spoke to him; and during the two days of his trial I listened carefully to the testimony of the witnesses who were called by the prosecution. On that basis I believe that Pinkhasov is innocent of the crimes charged.

6. Based upon what I observed at the trial, and upon the statements made by Judge Rasmasanov and by the other People's Assessor, I believe that Pinkhasov was prosecuted because he had made an application to emigrate to Israel. During a recess in the trial, I informed Pinkhasov's family that I had learned that the prosecution against him was a result of his application to emigrate. According to the judge, the prosecution would be dropped if Pinkhasov were to renounce his desire to go to Israel and were to persuade his wife and children to return to the U.S.S.R.

7. At the trial, Pinkhasov requested permission to call witnesses on his behalf but he was not permitted to do so by the judge.

8. The testimony of the witnesses called by the prosecution did not substantiate the charges.

9. At the conclusion of the trial, Judge Rasmasanov and the other People's Assessor prepared a guilty verdict which did not correspond to the testimony of the witnesses.

10. Judge Rasmasanov and the other People's Assessor decided to sentence Pinkhasov to seven years deprivation of freedom but I refused to sign the verdict which carried that sentence. When the judge and the other assessor agreed to a sentence of five years, I signed the verdict, as I believed that if I were to refuse to sign, another trial would inevitably result in the same verdict and a seven-year sentence.

11. After the trial, Pinkhasov's file was sent to Moscow, even though no appeal was taken there.

AFFIDAVIT OF SHIMON GRILIUS

1. My name is Shimon Grilius and I am a citizen of Israel, having emigrated from the Soviet Union on the first of December, 1974. I now reside in Holon, Israel.

2. In August 1974, I completed a five-year sentence of deprivation of freedom in a corrective-labor colony with a strict regime, under a verdict of the Judicial Board for Criminal Cases of the Ryazan District Court entered February 19, 1970.

3. In both labor colonies in which I served my sentence, I and the other Jewish prisoners were subjected to abuse and persecution because we were Jews. In both camps many of the prisoners were former Nazis, including many who were Germans. The Nazis co-operated with the camp authorities and were given the best positions for work. They assisted in the camp administration, including the distribution of food and the searching and watching of the living quarters. With the knowledge of the camp administration, the Nazi prisoners often harangued the Jewish prisoners and expressed virulent anti-Semitism.

4. In both camps, I and the other Jewish prisoners were prevented from observing the practices of our religion. We were prevented from wearing yarmulkas, from keeping beards, from studying our religion, and from maintaining a religious diet. Jewish prayerbooks and bibles and other written documents relating solely to the Jewish religion were confiscated. Our yarmulkas were confiscated, and we were repeatedly subjected to being forcibly shaved.

5. In January 1973, a procurator of the Perm *Oblast,* named

Miakishev, came to the Perm camps and made a ruling that the
Jewish prisoners would not be permitted to observe religious practices. Miakishev stated that the Declaration of Human Rights was
not intended for Jews, but only for Negroes, and that, although
Christians were allowed to have crosses, he had received no instructions that Jews were allowed to observe their religion.

6. I and my fellow Jewish prisoners were often punished for our
attempts to observe the rules of our religion.

7. At Perm, I was a fellow camp inmate of Yuri Vudka from
July 1972 until March 1973, when Vudka was transferred to Vladimir Prison under a sentence of prison confinement for the maximum term of three years. Prior to July 1972, Vudka was
incarcerated in the Mordovia Region, in the Potma labor camp
ZHKH 385/19, under a verdict of the Judicial Board for Criminal
Cases of the Ryazan District Court rendered on February 17, 1970,
sentencing him to seven years deprivation of freedom.

8. I have knowledge of the conditions of Vudka's confinement
in the camps from my own personal observations and from numerous conversations I had with Vudka while we were fellow campmates. I also have knowledge of his prison conditions in Vladimir
Prison from persons who were in Vladimir with Vudka.

9. Throughout his imprisonment in the camps, Vudka was subjected to persecution and punishment, both by Nazi prisoners and by
the camp administration, because he was a Jew and because he attempted to observe Jewish rules.

10. The following is a chronological outline of the many punishments that Vudka suffered while in the camps.

11. In Mordovia, in April or May 1972, after his entire unit was
late for dinner in the barracks dining room, he and one other Jewish prisoner, Yagman, were singled out for punishment. Vudka was
put into a punitive solitary cell for twelve days.

12. In June 1972, soon after Vudka exposed to his fellow prisoners the presence in the camp of Martimonov, who was the agent
provocateur who had denounced Vudka to the KGB, Vudka was
placed into PKT* for six months. Approximately a month after
Vudka began his PKT confinement, he, along with many other
prisoners, was transferred from Mordovia to Perm VS-389/36.
Other prisoners who had been in the PKT in Mordovia were allowed,
upon their transfer to Perm, to remain in the camp area. Vudka,
however, was immediately placed into the PKT at Perm to finish
his term of six months. He was informed by the camp administration
that there was a special instruction to place him in the PKT, but
there were no similar instructions concerning the other prisoners.

* Cell-type quarters.

13. During his detention in the PKT in Perm, Vudka was subjected to saltpeter in his food and was forced to take certain unknown pills. He experienced loss of dreams, loss of ejaculation, and began to feel apathy and sleepiness. After he protested, and other prisoners supported his protest, Vudka began to receive food which was not doctored with saltpeter.

14. On November 30, 1972, one day before Vudka's term of imprisonment in the PKT was to end, his brother, Valery Vudka, came to Perm to make a lengthy, authorized visit with his brother. Valery Vudka had traveled thousands of kilometers to see his brother before he departed for Israel. The visit was prevented, however, on the grounds that Vudka had committed three violations of regulations. The three alleged violations were as follows:

a. A red ballpoint pen was found in Vudka's possession. Such pens had previously been permitted to camp inmates and Vudka had possessed such a pen before he was placed in the PKT. However, while he was in the PKT, red ballpoint pens were forbidden and were taken away from the inmates. Vudka's red pen was not confiscated, however, and consequently he was found to be in violation of the new rule.

b. Vudka had asked his neighboring cellmate in the PKT to assist him in carrying out from his cell the heavy metal toilet bowl called the "parasha." This was considered a refusal to carry out an order given by an officer to take the "parasha" out, and consequently Vudka was found to be in violation of that order.

c. In accordance with the Safety Labor Rules of the camp, Vudka had requested mittens and felt boots for working outside in the cold. He had not received the required clothing and had thus been unable to go outside to work. Consequently, it was found that he had refused to go to work in violation of the camp regulations.

15. On November 30, 1972, the same day that his brother arrived to visit him and was prevented from making the visit, Vudka was assigned to work on the most difficult and dirtiest work in the barrack shop of the thermoelectric heaters. That shop does not have adequate ventilation for the work involved, and there is no possibility for the prisoner to wash in warm water after he finishes his shift. Vudka's supervisor in that shop was a Nazi criminal who had been a former supervisor in one of the Nazi concentration camps, either Buchenwald or Auschwitz. During his work in this job, Vudka was prevented from fulfilling his fixed norm because he was given a lesser number of components to work on than that which could satisfy the quota he was required to meet. Since he

was carrying out an operation that depended upon the preceding operations, he could not control the quantity of his work output. Consequently, his failure to meet his quota was not of his own volition.

16. On December 24, 1972, approximately a month after his release from the PKT, Vudka sent a statement to Podgorny, the Chairman of the Presidium of the Supreme Soviet of the U.S.S.R., asking for recognition of his Israeli citizenship and protesting against the political trials of Jews in the Soviet Union. He also requested that he and other political Jewish prisoners be released and allowed to emigrate to Israel. In the statement, Vudka protested further against the religious persecution to which he and his fellow Jewish prisoners were subjected.

17. In the early part of 1973, Vudka was subjected to an intensification of persecution and punishment. Because he had visited a Jewish comrade in the neighboring barracks without having received permission to do so, Vudka was deprived of the right to buy food products in the camp canteen for three months. During this period, Vudka was handcuffed, forcibly shaved, his yarmulka was torn from his head, and he was put into a punitive isolation cell. A group of former Nazi criminals called the "Soviet of the Collective" summoned Vudka and attempted to "educate" him, but Vudka refused to talk to such "educators."

18. Early in 1973, Vudka sent written complaints to the Union organs in Moscow, in which he protested the religious persecution to which he and his comrades were subjected and, also, complained about other unlawful conditions in the camp. He complained about the unlawful deprivation of his brother's visit, about his having been prevented from receiving visits from his other relatives, about the violations of the Safety Labor Regulations at work, about the absence of cotton-wool pants and felt boots permitted by law. The director of the VS-389 administration, Colonel Mikov, diverted these complaints and failed to send them to Moscow. Vudka learned of this diversion when Colonel Mikov himself began to answer Vudka's complaints in the name of the Union bodies. At that point, Vudka began to send complaints to Moscow, stating that Mikov was illegally preventing Vudka from making his protests directly to the proper higher bodies.

19. In March 1973, for having refused to remove his yarmulka, Vudka was punished by being placed in the SHIZO* for ten days. While incarcerated in the SHIZO, Vudka was handcuffed and forcibly shaved, and was then sentenced to an additional ten days in the SHIZO for having refused to shave himself. (According to camp

---

* Solitary confinement cell.

regulations the maximum time a prisoner can be kept in the SHIZO
is fifteen days.)

20. At the end of his incarceration in the SHIZO, Vudka was
brought to a room in which the following persons were present:
the judge of the People's Court of the city of Chusovaya, two
People's Assessors, the procurator from the Chusovaya region; the
head of the third unit of the camp, Lt. Dolmatov, and the guards
who accompanied Vudka. Vudka was informed that he would be
placed on trial immediately for his conduct in the camp.

21. Vudka later informed me personally that his "trial" in
March 1973 occurred in the following manner. Vudka addressed
the court in Hebrew and asked for a translator, but none was provided. Vudka was not given the charge sheet to read, nor any
access to a lawyer or anyone else who might have acted as his defense attorney. Lt Dolmatov spoke for thirty to forty minutes,
describing Vudka's failure to meet a fixed norm of work production
in the thermoelectric heater shop, Vudka's failure to pay attention
to educational measures, Vudka's failure to show any "improve-
ment" after being subjected to all forms of punishment, and Vudka's
"negative influence" on the other prisoners—an allegation that was
not explained in any way. When Dolmatov completed his address,
the procurator repeated word for word what Dolmatov had said.
The court then granted the petition of the camp administration to
transfer Vudka to a prison regime for the period of three years.
Pursuant to this decision, Vudka was transferred to Vladimir Prison.

22. While in Vladimir Prison, Vudka has been prevented from
receiving visits to which he is entitled by law. Vudka is married to
a woman named Anna Gurevich (although he was not permitted
to register his marriage after his arrest in 1969), but on November
19, 1974, Anna Gurevich was prevented from visiting Vudka in
prison at the authorized time. The prison officials informed her
that the reason she would be forbidden to see Vudka was that she
would not have a "positive influence" on him. Gurevich protested
to the procurator of the city of Vladimir, who informed her that
she would be permitted to see Vudka only if she pledged to persuade Vudka not to write complaints to Moscow.

23. While in Vladimir Prison, Vudka has been subjected to extremely harsh conditions. He has not received letters written to him
by his brother and other relatives and friends from Israel. He is
also suffering from an extremely poor diet and consequently his
health has deteriorated drastically. He is suffering from radiculitis
of the spine, which is exacerbated by the freezing conditions in his
cell. He continues to be subjected to religious persecution, including

forcible shaving, and prevention of the study of his religion. He has been subjected to physical attacks by other prisoners.

24. In both Mordovia and Perm I was a fellow campmate of Josif Mendelevich, who was confined under a sentence of the Leningrad City Court entered December 24, 1970, sentencing him, upon Supreme Court reduction, to twelve years deprivation of freedom in a labor colony of strict regime.

25. I have knowledge of the conditions of Mendelevich's confinement in the camps from my own personal observations and from numerous conversations I had with Mendelevich while we were fellow campmates.

26. Mendelevich has been in very poor physical health during his entire incarceration. He suffers from a high blood pressure condition and from a heart ailment which he had developed before his imprisonment. During the four years while he was my fellow campmate he was never given a medical checkup, despite instructions from the Medical Commission of the Department of the Interior of Permskaya *Oblast* Executive Committee. In September 1973 and in August 1974, that commission visited Camp VS-389/36 at Perm, where Mendelevich was then incarcerated and, after examination, concluded that Mendelevich should be sent to the hospital for a full medical checkup. Mendelevich was not so sent. When Mendelevich suffered attacks of high blood pressure, he was given no medication except for pain killers and was refused permission to stay out of work. His general poor health has resulted in his losing some of his teeth.

27. Mendelevich has been repeatedly and continuously subjected to punishment and persecution for his attempts to observe the religious practices of the Jewish religion. His beard has been forcibly shaved under threats that, if he resisted the shaving, he would be placed into the PKT or be transferred to the Vladimir Prison (both of which would be particularly dangerous for him because of his heart ailment). He has been punished for having attempted to wear a beard by being deprived of the right to buy food in the camp's shop. He has been repeatedly subjected to the forcible removal of his yarmulka and, in January 1973, the procurator of the Places of Detention of the Permskaya *Oblast,* Miakishev, ordered Mendelevich's yarmulka to be confiscated. Since that time, Mendelevich has worn a handkerchief as a head cover, but even that has been forcibly pulled off his head repeatedly.

28. All religious books which have been sent to Mendelevich have been confiscated. The Director of the Institute for Research of Truth in Paris, France, sent a copy of the bible to Mendelevich, but this was confiscated also. Relatives and friends have sent Mendelevich religious and Hebrew books, but he has not been per-

mitted to keep them. Mendelevich has been prevented from writing prayers in Hebrew, and a menorah which he carved from a piece of wood has been taken from him.

29. Mendelevich has attempted to observe the Jewish religion by prayer and by congregating with other Jewish prisoners on the Sabbath, but the camp administration has interfered with such attempts and threatened punishments for them.

30. Because of his religious beliefs, Mendelevich cannot eat pork, which is a regular part of the camp's diet. Since he is given no substitute for the pork, despite his requests, Mendelevich is deprived of an adequate diet for most of the year. In 1973 and 1974, for months before the Jewish holy day of Passover, Mendelevich and other Jewish prisoners in his camp at Perm appealed to the camp administration to be allowed to receive from relatives an amount of mazoth equivalent to the amount of bread normally allowed for the eight-day Passover observance. The request was refused, and the parcels of mazoth which were sent to the prisoners by their relatives were never received.

31. Letters written by Mendelevich to his parents in Riga and to his sisters in Israel are confiscated by the camp administration and never sent. In March and April 1974 he included in his letters comments regarding his suffering from the cold and from being physically ill; these letters were confiscated. Letters written to him from his relatives in Israel do not always reach him, and, when they do, it is usually after a great delay of two to four months. Mendelevich has been informed by the camp administration that his relatives should not write to him in Hebrew, and that if they wrote in Russian, the letters would arrive sooner.

32. Mendelevich has been subjected to physical attacks and other forms of persecution and anti-Semitic behavior by former Nazi criminals who are his campmates.

33. In June 1974, Mendelevich received three forms of punishment for a single violation of camp regulations. The punishment followed a protest conducted by more than forty political prisoners on June 23, 1973, in connection with the beating of a young Ukrainian Nationalist, Stepan Sapilyak, by a camp officer. The protest consisted of a refusal to go to work that day. As a result, Mendelevich was placed into the punishment ward for fifteen days, was deprived of the right to buy food products in the food shop for a month's period, and was deprived of the right to be visited by his parents.

34. Since 1971, every year on December 24, Mendelevich has sent to Podgorny, Chairman of the Presidium of the Supreme Soviet of the U.S.S.R., a protest in which he has asked to be recognized as an Israeli citizen, and has protested the persecution of the Jews.

E. Correspondence

The Honorable L. N. Smirnov
Judge of the Supreme Court of the R.S.F.S.R.
Moscow, U.S.S.R.

Dear Judge Smirnov:

I am hoping to travel to the Soviet Union in the near future and planning to be in Moscow from March 29 until about April 6. It is many years since we worked together at the Nuremberg War Crimes trials, and I would be very grateful for the opportunity to meet with you while I am in Moscow, to renew our acquaintance and discuss questions of mutual interest professionally.

With kindest personal regards, and in the hope of finding you in good health, I am

Sincerely yours,
TELFORD TAYLOR
Professor of Law

The Honorable Roman Rudenko
Procurator General of the U.S.S.R.
Moscow, U.S.S.R.

Dear General Rudenko:

I am hoping to travel to the Soviet Union in the near future and planning to be in Moscow from March 29 until about April 6. It is many years since we worked together at the Nuremberg War Crimes trials, and I would be very grateful for the opportunity to meet with you while I am in Moscow, to renew our acquaintance and discuss questions of mutual interest professionally.

With kindest personal regards, and in the hope of finding you in good health, I am

Sincerely yours,
TELFORD TAYLOR

April 12, 1974

The Honorable Roman A. Rudenko
Procurator General of the U.S.S.R.
Union Procuracy
Pushkinskaya
Moscow, U.S.S.R.

Dear General Rudenko:

I am most grateful for your thoughtfulness in making possible my visit to the Procuracy and my conference with Procurator Malyarov, who received me most courteously.

I very much regret that your illness made it impossible for me to meet with you, and hope that by now you are fully recovered.

With kindest personal regards,

Sincerely yours,
TELFORD TAYLOR
Professor of Law

April 12, 1974

M. P. Malyarov
First Deputy Procurator General of the U.S.S.R.
Union Procuracy
Pushkinskaya
Moscow, U.S.S.R.

Dear General Malyarov:

I am most grateful for the kind reception which you extended to me during my recent visit to Moscow, and for making so much time available to me.

I am likewise gratified by your assurance that the Procuracy will receive and consider the petitions which I soon will be submitting to you on behalf of the prisoners' relatives. Of course, I quite understand your point that the contents of these petitions will not become part of the records of the trials, and will be treated as addressed to the Procurator General's discretion.

With renewed thanks and kindest regards,

Sincerely yours,
TELFORD TAYLOR

June 10, 1974

R. A. Rudenko
Procurator General, U.S.S.R.

Dear General Rudenko:

On April 5, 1974, the First Deputy Procurator General was kind enough to give me permission to submit to the Procuracy a number of petitions from the wives and other relatives of certain Soviet citizens who had been convicted of various crimes and are now held in confinement. With this letter we respectfully submit these petitions to you, together with four auxiliary legal memoranda containing discussions of questions relating to a number of cases at once.

The legal memoranda and most of the petitions are submitted in both Russian and English. I must apologize for the fact that a shortage of Russian typewriters delayed us in the preparation of the Russian text of two of the petitions; I hope that we shall soon be in a position to submit these remaining petitions to you also in the Russian language.

Appended to each petition are the corresponding powers of attorney from relatives who have asked me to submit petitions in their behalf.

I am, needless to say, at your disposal and I should be happy to offer you any supplementary interpretation or explanation of whatever document interests you.

Permit me to express my deep gratitude for the opportunity afforded to me of presenting these petitions.

Very sincerely yours,

TELFORD TAYLOR
(Authorized Attorney
for the Petitioners)

July 7, 1974

Roman Andreyevich Rudenko
Procurator General, U.S.S.R.
Procuracy of the U.S.S.R.
Pushkinskaya Street
Moscow, U.S.S.R.

Dear General Rudenko:

Allow me to express my gratification and thanks for the courtesy and friendliness of our meeting last month. It was a great pleasure to see you again, and to find you in good health after so many years since our association at Nuremberg.

Unfortunately, I must also express my astonishment and sharp disappointment at the information given us by Deputy Procurator General Malyarov, when Professor Lipson telephoned him on June 18 to inquire whether we could be of any assistance in the review of our petitions, before our departure from Moscow. General Malyarov informed us, in effect, that he had no authority to depart from your instructions and that our petitions had already been denied.

This, of course, was quite contrary to the understanding which you and I had reached on June 12, that the petitions would be considered and that a written decision would be rendered.

On April 5 General Malyarov was kind enough to promise me that the Procuracy would receive the petitions. On June 12 you accepted the petitions and instructed Mr. Rogovin to transmit them to General Malyarov. To reject all the petitions without serious consideration of the factual basis and the legal arguments contained in them would be equivalent to not receiving them at all. Since there were nineteen petitions from three Soviet Republics (R.S.F.S.R., Moldavia, and Ukraine), it is obvious that by June 18 your staff could not possibly have examined the records in these cases and reviewed the allegations of our petitions with respect to illegal features of those proceedings.

I am especially distressed by the rejection of our request that you exercise your authority and responsibility as Procurator General to investigate the conditions under which the prisoners are held. When Professor Lipson asked General Malyarov about this matter, he received the reply that the Soviet system did not entertain requests for special treatment of individual prisoners. General Malyarov must have been misinformed about the contents of our petitions, which contained no requests for special treatment, but rather a request for an inquiry to determine whether the Soviet rules and principles for the custody of prisoners were being observed.

From every source of information it has been stated that, in the Soviet labor colonies, Jewish prisoners are confined with virulent anti-Semitic Nazi criminals, who are given favored treatment and harass and victimize the Jewish prisoners. Whether or not these allegations are true I do not know, but I am astonished that General Malyarov failed to reply at all responsibly to the affidavits and arguments on these matters. Surely you, as former Soviet Prosecutor at Nuremberg, are especially aware of the evils of anti-Semitism, and would be alert that it should not arise within the area of your own powers of supervision. No one, whether inside or outside the Soviet Union, will find it easy to understand how such a state of affairs could be permitted.

As you know from our conversation, our petitions also ask that

Article 64(a)—"High treason"—is an especially dangerous state crime. But is it possible to accuse a person of "high treason" who does not want to inflict this on his motherland, who does not consider himself to be a citizen of this country, to accuse a person who wanted to realize his right to leave, the right he was deprived of? I was acting according to the Soviet laws, applying to the Soviet offices for permission to leave the U.S.S.R., wasn't I? So why did the court absolutely ignore the circumstances, explaining the gist of the matter—the fact of my applying and the fact of the categorical refusal? In the indictment and in the verdict not a single word was mentioned about it. The Soviet Justice tried to make of us, me and my friends, a gang of maniacs, whose single aim was hijacking. As for Article 93—"Embezzlement of state or common property in especially large measures"—nothing is to be said at all, it is more than unsuitable. All the lawyers defending us at the trial announced a protest against it, and even the court did not try to accuse any of us of stealing the plane with the aim of profit. It was clear to everybody that the plane was a means of transportation. But nevertheless, only because in the Soviet Criminal Laws there was absent an article about hijacking at this time (it was introduced only in 1973), the court sentenced us according to an inappropriate article to quite large periods of prison.

The court did not take into consideration the fact that almost nothing happened, that the hijacking was only planned, and applied the case as though it was already carried out.

On June 15 it will be the fourth anniversary from the time my friends and I are suffering in the prison and camps. Four years of dirt, deprivation, insults, and offenses, hard forced labor. I think this is not the biggest payment for the hope to leave for Israel, to live at home. Even more can be suffered for that. But there must not be a shade of doubt about the character of those who take this payment, who day after day, drop after drop, drink our lives.

I shake hands with you with great respect

B. Penson
Mordovia, Lesnoe, spring 1974

P.S. I don't object to your using this letter in any useful form.

(Dear Paul Naumovich,
From your letter I found out about Mr. Taylor. If I have not understood everything in the right way, please correct my letter and send it to the destinee.

Yours, B Penson)

April 25, 1975

Mr. Josef Jakobi
4A Chissin Street
Entrance B, 4th Floor
Tel-Aviv, Israel

Dear Mr. Jakobi:

I am very grateful to you for sending me the letter from Mr. Penson. I will not ask how it was delivered, and needless to say it was a very moving experience to receive it. Unhappily, since there were no relatives of Mr. Penson in Israel, we have never been authorized to represent him. I think we can probably regard his letter now as authorization direct from him, and will see if any further action will be in any way helpful.

With renewed thanks,

Sincerely yours,
TELFORD TAYLOR

April 24, 1975

Mr. F. Tchernychev
TASS
883 National Press Building
Washington, D.C. 20045

Dear Mr. Tchernychev:

This is in reply to the questions which you recently transmitted to me by telephone, as follows:

1. What, in your view, is the significance of the Allied victory over Nazi Germany in World War II?
2. Would you please comment on the Soviet Army contribution to the victory?
3. What could you say about the cooperation of the U.S. and the Soviet Union in World War II, and what might be the importance of the cooperation between our two countries nowadays for prevention of a new World War?

With regard to your first question, there are of course many ways in which the defeat of Nazi Germany was of major significance in world history. The Allied victory spelled the end of Hitler's effort to dominate Europe and perhaps the world; it marked a great increase in the power and international responsibilities of both your country and mine; it revealed the full extent of the Nazi racial and other atrocities, including the killing of a large fraction of the Jewish people.

A NOTE ON THE TYPE

The text of this book was set on the Linotype in a face called
Times Roman, designed by Stanley Morison for *The Times* (London)
and first introduced by that newspaper in 1932.

Among typographers and designers of the twentieth century,
Stanley Morison has been a strong forming influence,
as a typographical adviser to the English Monotype Corporation,
as a director of two distinguished English publishing houses
and as a writer of sensibility, erudition, and keen practical sense.

This book was composed by American Book–Stratford Press,
Brattleboro, Vermont, and printed and bound by The Haddon
Craftsmen, Scranton, Pennsylvania.

Typography by Sidney Feinberg.